THE PATRIOTIC POEMS
OF
WALT WHITMAN

THE PATRIOTIC POEMS OF WALT WHITMAN

WALT WHITMAN

GYAN

Published by

Gyan Publishing House
5, Ansari Road
Daryaganj, New Delhi-110002
Phone: 011-47034999, 9811692060
E-mail: books@gyanbooks.com

Distribution Network
gyanbooks.com
India, USA, Canada, UK, Australia

ISBN: 978-93-6208-766-9 (PB)
First Published, 1918

2nd Impression 2024

Printed at: Gyan Press, Delhi.

THE PATRIOTIC POEMS OF WALT WHITMAN
Author: WALT WHITMAN

THE PATRIOTIC POEMS OF WALT WHITMAN

America

CENTRE of equal daughters, equal sons,
All, all alike, endear'd, grown, ungrown, young or old,
Strong, ample, fair, enduring, capable, rich,
Perennial with the Earth, with Freedom, Law and Love,
A grand, sane, towering, seated Mother,
Chair'd in the adamant of Time.

THE PATRIOTIC POEMS OF WALT WHITMAN

GARDEN CITY NEW YORK
DOUBLEDAY, PAGE & COMPANY
1918

ACKNOWLEDGMENT

This little volume of poems, selected from the complete edition published by us, is issued with the approval of the Whitman Executors, T. B. Harned and Horace Traubel, holders of the copyright. With one exception each poem here printed is complete.

The Publishers.

CONTENTS

CONTENTS

II. POEMS OF AFTER-WAR

III. POEMS OF AMERICA

IV. POEMS OF DEMOCRACY

CONTENTS

I

POEMS OF WAR

THICK-SPRINKLED BUNTING

THICK-SPRINKLED bunting! flag of stars!
Long yet your road, fateful flag—long yet your road, and lined with bloody death,
For the prize I see at issue at last is the world,
All its ships and shores I see interwoven with your threads greedy banner;
Dream'd again the flags of kings, highest borne, to flaunt unrival'd?
O hasten flag of man—O with sure and steady step, passing highest flags of kings,
Walk supreme to the heavens mighty symbol—run up above them all,
Flag of stars! thick-sprinkled bunting!

BEAT! BEAT! DRUMS!

Beat! beat! drums!—blow! bugles! blow!
Through the windows—through doors—burst like a ruthless force,
Into the solemn church, and scatter the congregation,
Into the school where the scholar is studying;
Leave not the bridegroom quiet—no happiness must he have now with his bride,
Not the peaceful farmer any peace, ploughing his field or gathering his grain,
So fierce you whirr and pound you drums—so shrill you bugles blow.

Beat! beat! drums!—blow! bugles! blow!
Over the traffic of cities—over the rumble of wheels in the streets;
Are beds prepared for sleepers at night in the houses? no sleepers must sleep in those beds,
No bargainers' bargains by day—no brokers or speculators—would they continue?
Would the talkers be talking? would the singer attempt to sing?
Would the lawyer rise in the court to state his case before the judge?
Then rattle quicker, heavier drums—you bugles wilder blow.

Walt Whitman

Beat! beat! drums!—blow! bugles! blow!
Make no parley—stop for no expostulation,
Mind not the timid—mind not the weeper or prayer,
Mind not the old man beseeching the young man,
Let not the child's voice be heard, nor the mother's
entreaties,
Make even the trestles to shake the dead where they
lie awaiting the hearses,
So strong you thump O terrible drums—so loud you
bugles blow.

CITY OF SHIPS

City of ships!
(O the black ships! O the fierce ships!
O the beautiful sharp-bow'd steam-ships and sail-ships!)
City of the world! (for all races are here,
All the lands of the earth make contributions here);
City of the sea! city of hurried and glittering tides!
City whose gleeful tides continually rush or recede, whirling in and out with eddies and foam!
City of wharves and stores—city of tall façades of marble and iron!
Proud and passionate city—mettlesome, mad, extravagant city!
Spring up O city—not for peace alone, but be indeed yourself, warlike!
Fear not—submit to no models but your own O,city!
Behold me—incarnate me as I have incarnated you!

I have rejected nothing you offer'd me—whom you adopted I have adopted,
Good or bad I never question you—I love all—I do not condemn anything,
I chant and celebrate all that is yours—yet peace no more,
In peace I chanted peace, but now the drum of war is mine,
War, red war is my song through your streets, O city!

Walt Whitman

A MARCH IN THE RANKS HARD-PREST, AND THE ROAD UNKNOWN

A MARCH in the ranks hard-prest, and the road unknown,
A route through a heavy wood with muffled steps in the darkness,
Our army foil'd with loss severe, and the sullen remnant retreating,
Till after midnight glimmer upon us the lights of a dim-lighted building,
We come to an open space in the woods, and halt by the dim-lighted building,
'Tis a large old church at the crossing roads, now an impromptu hospital,
Entering but for a minute I see a sight beyond all the pictures and poems ever made,
Shadows of deepest, deepest black, just lit by moving candles and lamps,
And by one great pitchy torch stationary with wild red flame and clouds of smoke,
By these, crowds, groups of forms vaguely I see on the floor, some in the pews laid down,
At my feet more distinctly a soldier, a mere lad, in danger of bleeding to death (he is shot in the abdomen),
I stanch the blood temporarily (the youngster's face is white as a lily),

Then before I depart I sweep my eyes o'er the scene
 fain to absorb it all,
Faces, varieties, postures beyond description, most
 in obscurity, some of them dead,
Surgeons operating, attendants holding lights, the
 smell of ether, the odour of blood,
The crowd, O the crowd of the bloody forms, the
 yard outside also fill'd,
Some on the bare ground, some on planks or stretch-
 ers, some in the death-spasm sweating,
An occasional scream or cry, the doctor's shouted
 orders or calls,
The glisten of the little steel instruments catching
 the glint of the torches,
These I resume as I chant, I see again the forms, I
 smell the odour,
Then hear outside the orders given, *Fall in, my men,
 fall in;*
But first I bend to the dying lad, his eyes open, a half-
 smile gives he me,
Then the eyes close, calmly close, and I speed forth
 to the darkness,
Resuming, marching, ever in darkness marching,
 on in the ranks,
The unknown road still marching.

Walt Whitman

COME UP FROM THE FIELDS FATHER

Come up from the fields father, here's a letter from our Pete,
And come to the front door mother, here's a letter from thy dear son.

Lo, 'tis autumn,
Lo, where the trees, deeper green, yellower and redder,
Cool and sweeten Ohio's villages with leaves fluttering in the moderate wind,
Where apples ripe in the orchards hang and grapes on the trellis'd vines
(Smell you the smell of the grapes on the vines?
Smell you the buckwheat where the bees were lately buzzing?),
Above all, lo, the sky so calm, so transparent after the rain, and with wondrous clouds,
Below too, all calm, all vital and beautiful, and the farm prospers well.

Down in the fields all prospers well,
But now from the fields come father, come at the daughter's call,
And come to the entry mother, to the front door come right away.

Fast as she can she hurries, something ominous, her steps trembling,
She does not tarry to smooth her hair nor adjust her cap.

Open the envelope quickly,
O this is not our son's writing, yet his name is sign'd,
O a strange hand writes for our dear son, O stricken mother's soul!
All swims before her eyes, flashes with black, she catches the main words only,
Sentences broken, *gunshot wound in the breast, cavalry skirmish, taken to hospital,*
At present low, but will soon be better.

Ah now the single figure to me,
Amid all teeming and wealthy Ohio with all its cities and farms,
Sickly white in the face and dull in the head, very faint,
By the jamb of a door leans.

Grieve not so, dear mother (the just-grown daughter speaks through her sobs,
The little sisters huddle around speechless and dis-may'd),
See, dearest mother, the letter says Pete will soon be better.

Walt Whitman

Alas poor boy, he will never be better (nor may be needs to be better, that brave and simple soul),
While they stand at home at the door he is dead already,
The only son is dead.

But the mother needs to be better,
She with thin form presently drest in black,
By day her meals untouch'd, then at night fitfully sleeping, often waking,
In the midnight waking, weeping, longing with one deep longing,
O that she might withdraw unnoticed, silent from life escape and withdraw,
To follow, to seek, to be with her dear dead son.

A TWILIGHT SONG

As I sit in twilight late alone by the flickering oak-
flame,
Musing on long-pass'd war-scenes—of the countless
buried unknown soldiers,
Of the vacant names, as unindented air's and sea's—
the unreturn'd,
The brief truce after battle, with grim burial-squads,
and the deep-fill'd trenches
Of gather'd dead from all America, North, South,
East, West, whence they came up,
From wooded Maine, New-England's farms, from
fertile Pennsylvania, Illinois, Ohio,
From the measureless West, Virginia, the South, the
Carolinas, Texas
(Even here in my room-shadows and half-lights in
the noiseless flickering flames,
Again I see the stalwart ranks on-filing, ris-
ing—I hear the rhythmic tramp of the
armies);
You million unwrit names all, all—you dark bequest
from all the war,
A special verse for you—a flash of duty long neg-
lected—your mystic roll strangely gather'd
here,
Each name recall'd by me from out the darkness
and death's ashes,

Henceforth to be, deep, deep within my heart recording, for many a future year,
Your mystic roll entire of unknown names, or North or South,
Embalm'd with love in this twilight song.

A SIGHT IN CAMP IN THE DAYBREAK GRAY AND DIM

A SIGHT in camp in the daybreak gray and dim,
As from my tent I emerge so early sleepless,
As slow I walk in the cool fresh air the path near by the hospital tent,
Three forms I see on stretchers lying, brought out there untended lying,
Over each the blanket spread, ample brownish woollen blanket,
Gray and heavy blanket, folding, covering all.

Curious I halt and silent stand,
Then with light fingers I from the face of the nearest the first just lift the blanket;
Who are you elderly man so gaunt and grim, with well-gray'd hair, and flesh all sunken about the eyes?
Who are you my dear comrade?

Then to the second I step—and who are you my child and darling?
Who are you sweet boy with cheeks yet blooming?

Then to the third—a face nor child nor old, very calm, as of beautiful yellow-white ivory;

Walt Whitman

Young man I think I know you—I think this face is the face of the Christ himself,
Dead and divine and brother of all, and here again he lies.

YEAR THAT TREMBLED AND REEL'D BENEATH ME

YEAR that trembled and reel'd beneath me!
Your summer wind was warm enough, yet the air I breathed froze me,
A thick gloom fell through the sunshine and darken'd me,
Must I change my triumphant songs? said I to myself,
Must I indeed learn to chant the cold dirges of the baffled,
And sullen hymns of defeat?

FIRST O SONGS FOR A PRELUDE

First O songs for a prelude,
Lightly strike on the stretch'd tympanum pride and joy in my city,
How she led the rest to arms, how she gave the cue,
How at once with lithe limbs unwaiting a moment she sprang,
(O superb! O Manhattan, my own, my peerless.
O strongest you in the hour of danger, in crisis! O truer than steel!)
How you sprang—how you threw off the costumes of peace with indifferent hand,
How your soft opera-music changed, and the drum and fife were heard in their stead,
How you led to the war (that shall serve for our prelude, songs of soldiers),
How Manhattan drum-taps led.

Forty years had I in my city seen soldiers parading,
Forty years as a pageant, till unawares the lady of this teeming and turbulent city,
Sleepless amid her ships, her houses, her incalculable wealth,
With her million children around her, suddenly,
At dead of night, at news from the south,
Incens'd struck with clinch'd hand the pavement.

A shock electric, the night sustain'd it,
Till with ominous hum our hive at daybreak pour'd out its myriads.
From the houses then and the workshops, and through all the doorways,
Leapt they tumultuous, and lo! Manhattan arming.

To the drum-taps prompt,
The young men falling in and arming,
The mechanics arming (the trowel, the jack-plane, the blacksmith's hammer, tost aside with precipitation),
The lawyer leaving his office and arming, the judge leaving the court,
The driver deserting his wagon in the street, jumping down, throwing the reins abruptly down on the horses' backs,
The salesman leaving the store, the boss, book-keeper, porter, all leaving;
Squads gather everywhere by common consent and arm,
The new recruits, even boys, the old men show them how to wear their accoutrements, they buckle the straps carefully,
Outdoors arming, indoors arming, the flash of the musket-barrels,
The white tents cluster in camps, the arm'd sentries around, the sunrise cannon and again at sunset,

Arm'd regiments arrive every day, pass through the
city, and embark from the wharves
(How good they look as they tramp down to the river,
sweaty, with their guns on their shoulders!
How I love them! how I could hug them, with
their brown faces and their clothes and knap-
sacks cover'd with dust!)
The blood of the city up—arm'd! arm'd! the
cry everywhere,
The flags flung out from the steeples of churches
and from all the public buildings and stores,
The tearful parting, the mother kisses her son, the
son kisses his mother
(Loth is the mother to part, yet not a word does she
speak to detain him),
The tumultuous escort, the ranks of policemen
preceding, clearing the way,
The unpent enthusiasm, the wild cheers of the
crowd for their favourites,
The artillery, the silent cannons bright as gold,
drawn along, rumble lightly over the stones
(Silent cannons, soon to cease your silence,
Soon unlimber'd to begin the red business);
All the mutter of preparation, all the determin'd
arming,
The hospital service, the lint, bandages, and medicines,
The women volunteering for nurses, the work begun
for in earnest, no mere parade now;

War! an arm'd race is advancing. the welcome
for battle, no turning away;
War! be it weeks, months, or years, an arm'd race
is advancing to welcome it

Mannahatta a-march—and it's O to sing it well!
It's O for a manly life in the camp.

And the sturdy artillery
The guns bright as gold, the work for giants, to
serve well the guns,
Unlimber them! (No more as the past torty years
for salutes for courtesies merely,
Put in something now besides powder and wadding.)

And you lady of ships, you Mannahatta,
Old matron of this proud, friendly, turbulent city,
Often in peace and wealth you were pensive or cov-
ertly frown'd amid all your children,
But now you smile with joy exulting old Manna-
hatta.

Walt Whitman

SONG OF THE BANNER AT DAYBREAK

Poet

O A NEW song, a free song,
Flapping, flapping, flapping, flapping, by sounds, by voices clearer,
By the wind's voice and that of the drum,
By the banner's voice and the child's voice and sea's voice and father's voice,
Low on the ground and high in the air,
On the ground where father and child stand,
In the upward air where their eyes turn,
Where the banner at daybreak is flapping,.

Words! book-words! what are you?
Words no more, for hearken and see,
My song is there in the open air, and I must sing,
With the banner and pennant a-flapping.

I'll weave the chord and twine in,
Man's desire and babe's desire, I'll twine them in, I'll put in life,
I'll put the bayonet's flashing point, I'll let bullets and slugs whizz
(As one carrying a symbol and menace far into the future,
Crying with trumpet voice, *Arouse and beware! Beware and arouse!*)

I'll pour the verse with streams of blood, full of volition, full of joy,
Then loosen, launch forth, to go and compete,
With the banner and pennant a-flapping.

Pennant

Come up here, bard, bard,
Come up here, soul, soul,
Come up here, dear little child,
To fly in the clouds and winds with me, and play with the measureless light.

Child

Father what is that in the sky beckoning to me with long finger?
And what does it say to me all the while?

Father

Nothing my babe you see in the sky,
And nothing at all to you it says—but look you my babe,
Look at these dazzling things in the houses, and see you the money-shops opening,
And see you the vehicles preparing to crawl along the streets with goods;
These, ah these, how valued and toil'd for these!
How envied by all the earth!

Walt Whitman

Poet

Fresh and rosy red the sun is mounting high,
On floats the sea in distant blue careering through
    its channels,
On floats the wind over the breast of the sea setting
    in toward land,
The great steady wind from west to west-by-south,
Floating so buoyant with milk-white foam on the
    waters.
But I am not the sea nor the red sun,
I am not the wind with girlish laughter,
Not the immense wind which strengthens, not the
    wind which lashes,
Not the spirit that ever lashes its own body to terror
    and death,
But I am that which unseen comes and sings, sings,
    sings,
Which babbles in brooks and scoots in showers on the
    land,
Which the birds know in the woods mornings and
    evenings,
And the shore-sands know and the hissing wave, and
    that banner and pennant,
Aloft there flapping and flapping.

Child

O father it is alive—it is full of people—it has chil-
    dren,

O now it seems to me it is talking to its children,
I hear it—it talks to me—O it is wonderful!
O it stretches—it spreads and runs so fast—O my father,
It is so broad it covers the whole sky.

Father

Cease, cease, my foolish babe,
What you are saying is sorrowful to me, much it displeases me;
Behold with the rest again I say, behold not banners and pennants aloft,
But the well-prepared pavements behold, and mark the solid-wall'd houses.

Banner and Pennant

Speak to the child O bard out of Manhattan,
To our children all, or north or south of Manhattan,
Point this day, leaving all the rest, to us over all—and yet we know not why,
For what are we, mere strips of cloth profiting nothing,
Only flapping in the wind?

Poet

I hear and see not strips of cloth alone,
I hear the tramp of armies, I hear the challenging sentry,

I hear the jubilant shouts of millions of men, I
hear Liberty!
I hear the drums beat and the trumpets blowing,
I myself move abroad swift-rising flying then,
I use the wings of the land-bird and use the wings of
the sea-bird, and look down as from a height,
I do not deny the precious results of peace, I see
populous cities with wealth incalculable,
I see numberless farms, I see the farmers working
in their fields or barns,
I see mechanics working, I see buildings everywhere
founded, going up, or finish'd,
I see trains of cars swiftly speeding along railroad
tracks drawn by the locomotives,
I see the stores, depots, of Boston, Baltimore,
Charleston, New Orleans,
I see far in the West the immense area of grain, I
dwell awhile hovering,
I pass to the lumber forests of the North, and again
to the Southern plantation, and again to
California;
Sweeping the whole I see the countless profit, the
busy gatherings, earn'd wages,
See the Identity formed out of thirty-eight spacious
and haughty States (and many more to
come),
See forts on the shores of harbours, see ships sailing
in and out;

Then over all (aye! aye!) my little and lengthen'd pennant shaped like a sword,
Runs swiftly up indicating war and defiance—and now the halyards have rais'd it,
Side of my banner broad and blue, side of my starry banner,
Discarding peace over all the sea and land.

Banner and Pennant

Yet louder, higher, stronger, bard! yet farther, wider cleave!
No longer let our children deem us riches and peace alone,
We may be terror and carnage, and are so now,
Not now are we any one of these spacious and haughty States (nor any five, nor ten),
Nor market nor depot we, nor money-bank in the city,
But these and all, and the brown and spreading land, and the mines below, are ours,
And the shores of the sea are ours, and the rivers great and small,
And the fields they moisten, and the crops and the fruits are ours,
Bays and channels and ships sailing in and out are ours—while we over all,
Over the area spread below, the three or four millions of square miles, the capitals,

The forty millions of people—O bard! in life and
    death supreme,
We, even we, henceforth flaunt out masterful, high
    up above,
Not for the present alone, for a thousand years
    chanting through you,
This song to the soul of one poor little child.

Child

O my father I like not the houses,
They will never to me be anything, nor do I like
    money,
But to mount up there I would like, O father dear,
    that banner I like,
That pennant I would be and must be.

Father

Child of mine you fill me with anguish,
To be that pennant would be too fearful,
Little you know what it is this day, and after this
    day, forever,
It is to gain nothing, but risk and defy every-
    thing,
Forward to stand in front of wars—and O, such
    wars!—what have you to do with them?
With passions of demons, slaughter, premature
    death?

Banner

Demons and death then I sing,
Put in all, aye all will I, sword-shaped pennant for
war,
And a pleasure new and ecstatic, and the prattled
yearning of children,
Blent with the sounds of the peaceful land and the
liquid wash of the sea,
And the black ships fighting on the sea envelop'd
in smoke,
And the icy cool of the far, far north, with rustling
cedars and pines,
And the whirr of drums and the sound of soldiers
marching, and the hot sun shining south,
And the beach-waves combing over the beach on
my Eastern shore, and my Western shore
the same,
And all between those shores, and my ever running
Mississippi with bends and chutes,
And my Illinois fields, and my Kansas fields, and
my fields of Missouri,
The Continent, devoting the whole identity without
reserving an atom,
Pour in! whelm that which asks, which sings, with
all and the yield of all,
Fusing and holding, claiming, devouring the
whole,
No more with tender lip, nor musical labial sound,

But out of the night emerging for food, our voice
persuasive no more,
Croaking like crows here in the wind.

Poet

My limbs, my veins dilate, my theme is clear at last,
Banner so broad advancing out of the night, I sing
you haughty and resolute,
I burst through where I waited long, too long, deaf-
en'd and blinded,
My hearing and tongue are come to me (a little
child taught me),
I hear from above O pennant of war your ironical
call and demand,
Insensate! insensate (yet I at any rate chant you),
O banner!
Not houses of peace indeed are you, nor any nor
all their prosperity (if need be, you shall
again have every one of those houses to de-
stroy them.
You thought not to destroy those valuable houses,
standing fast, full of comfort, built with
money,
May they stand fast, then? not an hour except
you above them and all stand fast);
O banner, not money so precious are you, not farm
produce you, nor the material good nutri-
ment,

Nor excellent stores, nor landed on wharves from
the ships,
Not the superb ships with sail-power or steam-
power, fetching and carrying cargoes,
Nor machinery, vehicles, trade, nor revenues—but
you as henceforth I see you,
Running up out of the night, bringing your cluster
of stars (ever-enlarging stars),
Divider of daybreak you, cutting the air, touch'd
by the sun, measuring the sky,
(Passionately seen and yearn'd for by one poor
little child,
While others remain busy or smartly talking, for-
ever teaching thrift, thrift);
O you up there! O pennant! where you undulate
like a snake hissing so curious,
Out of reach, an idea only, yet furiously fought for,
risking bloody death, loved by me,
So loved—O you banner leading the day with stars
brought from the night!
Valueless, object of eyes, over all and demanding
all—(absolute owner of all)—O banner and
pennant!
I too leave the rest!—great as it is, it is nothing—
houses, machines are nothing—I see them not.
I see but you, O warlike pennant! O banner so
broad, with stripes, I sing you only,
Flapping up there in the wind.

THE DYING VETERAN

(A Long Island incident—early part of the nineteenth century.)

AMID these days of order, ease, prosperity,
Amid the current songs of beauty, peace, decorum,
I cast a reminiscence—(likely 't will offend you,
I heard it in my boyhood)—More than a generation since,
A queer old savage man, a fighter under Washington himself
(Large, brave, cleanly, hot-blooded, no talker, rather spiritualistic,
Had fought in the ranks—fought well—had been all through the Revolutionary war),
Lay dying—sons, daughters, church-deacons, lovingly tending him,
Sharping their sense, their ears, towards his murmuring, half-caught words:
"Let me return again to my war-days,
To the sights and scenes—to forming the line of battle,
To the scouts ahead reconnoitering,
To the cannons, the grim artillery,
To the galloping aids, carrying orders,
To the wounded, the fallen, the heat, the suspense,
The perfume strong, the smoke, the deafening noise;
Away with your life of peace!—your joys of peace!
Give me my old wild battle-life again!"

THE WOUND-DRESSER

I

An old man bending I come among new faces,
Years looking backward resuming in answer to children,
Come tell us old man, as from young men and maidens that love me
(Arous'd and angry, I'd thought to beat the alarum, and urge relentless war,
But soon my fingers fail'd me, my face droop'd and I resign'd myself,
To sit by the wounded and soothe them, or silently watch the dead);
Years hence of these scenes, of these furious passions, these chances,
Of unsurpass'd heroes (was one side so brave? the other was equally brave);
Now be witness again, paint the mightiest armies of earth,
Of those armies so rapid so wondrous what saw you to tell us?
What stays with you latest and deepest? of curious panics,
Of hard-fought engagements or sieges tremendous what deepest remains?

2

O maidens and young men I love and that love me,
What you ask of my days those the strangest and sudden your talking recalls,
Soldier alert I arrive after a long march cover'd with sweat and dust,
In the nick of time I come, plunge in the fight, loudly shout in the rush of successful charge,
Enter the captur'd works—yet lo, like a swift-running river they fade,
Pass and are gone they fade—I dwell not on soldiers' perils or soldiers' joys
(Both I remember well—many the hardships, few the joys, yet I was content).

But in silence, in dreams' projections,
While the world of gain and appearance and mirth goes on,
So soon what is over forgotten, and waves wash the imprints off the sand,
With hinged knees returning I enter the doors (while for you up there,
Whoever you are, follow without noise and be of strong heart).

Bearing the bandages, water and sponge,
Straight and swift to my wounded I go,

Where they lie on the ground after the battle brought
in,
Where their priceless blood reddens the grass, the
ground,
Or to the rows of the hospital tent, or under the
roof'd hospital,
To the long rows of cots up and down each side I
return,
To each and all one after another I draw near, not
one do I miss,
An attendant follows holding a tray, he carries a
refuse pail,
Soon to be fill'd with clotted rags and blood, emp-
tied, and fill'd again.

I onward go, I stop,
With hinged knees and steady hand to dress wounds,
I am firm with each, the pangs are sharp yet unavoid-
able,
One turns to me his appealing eyes—poor boy!
I never knew you,
Yet I think I could not refuse this moment to die
for you, if that would save you.

3

On, on I go (open doors of time! open hospital doors!)
The crush'd head I dress (poor crazed hand tear
not the bandage away),

The neck of the cavalry-man with the bullet through
and through I examine,
Hard the breathing rattles, quite glazed already the
eye, yet life struggles hard,
(Come sweet death! be persuaded O beautiful
death!
In mercy come quickly).

From the stump of the arm, the amputated hand,
I undo the clotted lint, remove the slough, wash off
the matter and blood,
Back on his pillow the soldier bends with curv'd
neck and side-falling head,
His eyes are closed, his face is pale, he dares not
look on the bloody stump,
And has not yet look'd on it.

I dress a wound in the side, deep, deep,
But a day or two more, for see the frame all wasted
and sinking,
And the yellow-blue countenance see.

I dress the perforated shoulder, the foot with the
bullet-wound,
Cleanse the one with a gnawing and putrid gangrene,
so sickening, so offensive,
While the attendant stands behind aside me holding
the tray and pail.

I am faithful, I do not give out,
The fractur'd thigh, the knee, the wound in the abdomen,
These and more I dress with impassive hand (yet deep in my breast a fire, a burning flame).

4

Thus in silence in dreams' projections,
Returning, resuming, I thread my way through the hospitals,
The hurt and wounded I pacify with soothing hand,
I sit by the restless all the dark night, some are so young,
Some suffer so much, I recall the experience sweet and sad
(Many a soldier's loving arms about this neck have cross'd and rested,
Many a soldier's kiss dwells on these bearded lips).

Walt Whitman

DIRGE FOR TWO VETERANS

THE last sunbeam
Lightly falls from the finish'd Sabbath,
On the pavement here, and there beyond it is looking
Down a new-made double grave

Lo, the moon ascending,
Up from the east the silvery round moon,
Beautiful over the house-tops, ghastly, phantom moon,
Immense and silent moon.

I see a sad procession,
And I hear the sound of coming full-key'd bugles,
All the channels of the city streets they're flooding,
As with voices and with tears.

I hear the great drums pounding,
And the small drums steady whirring,
And every blow of the great convulsive drums,
Strikes me through and through.

For the son is brought with the father
(In the foremost ranks of the fierce assault they fell,
Two veterans, son and father, dropt together,
And the double grave awaits them).

Now nearer blow the bugles,
And the drums strike more convulsive,
And the daylight over the pavement quite has faded,
And the strong dead-march enwraps me.

In the eastern sky up-buoying,
The sorrowful vast phantom moves illumin'd
('Tis some mother's large transparent face,
In heaven brighter growing).

O strong dead-march you please me!
O moon immense with your silvery face you soothe me!
O my soldiers twain! O my veterans passing to burial!
What I have I also give you.

The moon gives you light,
And the bugles and the drums give you music,
And my heart, O my soldiers, my veterans,
My heart gives you love.

FROM FAR DAKOTA'S CAÑONS

June 25, 1876.

FROM far Dakota's cañons,
Lands of the wild ravine, the dusky Sioux, the lonesome stretch, the silence,
Haply to-day a mournful wail, haply a trumpet-note for heroes.

The battle-bulletin,
The Indian ambuscade, the craft, the fatal environment,
The cavalry companies fighting to the last in sternest heroism,
In the midst of their little circle, with their slaughter'd horses for breastworks,
The fall of Custer and all his officers and men.

Continues yet the old, old legend of our race,
The loftiest of life upheld by death,
The ancient banner perfectly maintain'd,
O lesson opportune, O how I welcome thee!

As sitting in dark days,
Lone, sulky, through the time's thick murk looking in vain for light, for hope,
From unsuspected parts a fierce and momentary proof

(The sun there at the centre though conceal'd,
Electric life forever at the centre),
Breaks forth a lightning flash.

Thou of the tawny flowing hair in battle,
I erewhile saw, with erect head, pressing ever in front, bearing a bright sword in thy hand,
Now ending well in death the splendid fever of thy deeds
(I bring no dirge for it or thee, I bring a glad triumphal sonnet),
Desperate and glorious, aye in defeat most desperate, most glorious,
After thy many battles in which never yielding up a gun or a colour,
Leaving behind thee a memory sweet to soldiers,
Thou yieldest up thyself.

OLD WAR-DREAMS

In midnight sleep of many a face of anguish,
Of the look at first of the mortally wounded (of
 that indescribable look),
Of the dead on their backs with arms extended wide,
 I dream, I dream, I dream.

Of scenes of Nature, fields and mountains,
Of skies so beauteous after a storm, and at night
 the moon so unearthly bright,
Shining sweetly, shining down, where we dig the
 trenches and gather the heaps,
 I dream, I dream, I dream.

Long have they pass'd, faces and trenches and fields,
Where through the carnage I moved with a callous
 composure, or away from the fallen,
Onward I sped at the time—but now of their forms
 at night,
 I dream, I dream, I dream.

DELICATE CLUSTER

DELICATE cluster! flag of teeming life!
Covering all my lands—all my seashores lining!
Flag of death! (how I watch'd you through the smoke of battle pressing!
How I heard you flap and rustle, cloth defiant!)
Flag cerulean—sunny flag, with the orbs of night dappled!
Ah my silvery beauty—ah my woolly white and crimson!
Ah to sing the song of you, my matron mighty!
My sacred one, my mother!

Walt Whitman

TO A CERTAIN CIVILIAN

Did you ask dulcet rhymes from me?
Did you seek the civilian's peaceful and languishing rhymes?
Did you find what I sang erewhile so hard to follow?
Why I was not singing erewhile for you to follow, to understand—nor am I now;
(I have been born of the same as the war was born,
The drum-corps' rattle is ever to me sweet music, I love well the martial dirge,
With slow wail and convulsive throb leading the officer's funeral);
What to such as you anyhow such a poet as I? therefore leave my works,
And go lull yourself with what you can understand, and with piano-tunes,
For I lull nobody, and you will never understand me.

ADIEU TO A SOLDIER

Adieu O soldier,
You of the rude campaigning (which we shared),
The rapid march, the life of the camp,
The hot contention of opposing fronts, the long manœuvre,
Red battles with their slaughter, the stimulus, the strong terrific game,
Spell of all brave and manly hearts, the trains of time through you and like of you all fill'd,
With war and war's expression.

Adieu dear comrade,
Your mission is fulfill'd—but I, more warlike,
Myself and this contentious soul of mine,
Still on our own campaigning bound,
Through untried roads with ambushes opponents lined,
Through many a sharp defeat and many a crisis, often baffled,
Here marching, ever marching on, a war fight out—aye here,
To fiercer, weightier battles give expression.

LONG, TOO LONG AMERICA

LONG, too long America,
Travelling roads all even and peaceful you learn'd from joys and prosperity only,
But now, ah now, to learn from crises of anguish, advancing, grappling with direst fate and recoiling not,
And now to conceive and show to the world what your children en-masse really are.
(For who except myself has yet conceiv'd what your children en-masse really are?).

II

POEMS OF AFTER-WAR

WEAVE IN, MY HARDY LIFE

WEAVE in, weave in, my hardy life,
Weave yet a soldier strong and full for great campaigns to come,
Weave in red blood, weave sinews in like ropes, the senses, sight weave in,
Weave lasting sure, weave day and night the weft, the warp, incessant weave, tire not
(We know not what the use O life, nor know the aim, the end, nor really aught we know,
But know the work, the need goes on and shall go on, the death-envelop'd march of peace as well as war goes on),
For great campaigns of peace the same the wiry threads to weave,
We know not why or what, yet weave, forever weave.

HOW SOLEMN AS ONE BY ONE

(Washington City, 1865)

How solemn as one by one,
As the ranks returning worn and sweaty, as the men file by where I stand,
As the faces the masks appear, as I glance at the faces studying the masks
(As I glance upward out of this page studying you, dear friend, whoever you are),
How solemn the thought of my whispering soul to each in the ranks, and to you!
I see behind each mask that wonder a kindred soul,
O the bullet could never kill what you really are, dear friend,
Nor the bayonet stab what you really are;
The soul! yourself I see, great as any, good as the best,
Waiting secure and content, which the bullet could never kill,
Nor the bayonet stab O friend.

Walt Whitman

SPIRIT WHOSE WORK IS DONE

(Washington City, 1865)

SPIRIT whose work is done—spirit of dreadful hours!
Ere departing fade from my eyes your forests of bayonets;
Spirit of gloomiest fears and doubts (yet onward evèr unfaltering pressing),
Spirit of many a solemn day and many a savage scene—electric spirit,
That with muttering voice through the war now closed, like a tireless phantom flitted,
Rousing the land with breath of flame, while you beat and beat the drum,
Now as the sound of the drum, hollow and harsh to the last, reverberates round me,
As your ranks, your immortal ranks, return, return from the battles,
As the muskets of the young men yet lean over their shoulders,
As I look on the bayonets bristling over their shoulders,
As those slanted bayonets, whole forests of them appearing in the distance, approach and pass on, returning homeward,
Moving with steady motion, swaying to and fro to the right and left,

Evenly, lightly rising and falling while the steps keep
time;
Spirit of hours I knew, all hectic red one day, but
pale as death next day,
Touch my mouth ere you depart, press my lips close,
Leave me your pulses of rage—bequeath them to me
—fill me with currents convulsive,
Let them scorch and blister out of my chants when
you are gone,
Let them identify you to the future in these songs.

Walt Whitman

THE RETURN OF THE HEROES

1

For the lands and for these passionate days and for
myself,
Now I awhile retire to thee O soil of autumn fields,
Reclining on thy breast, giving myself to thee,
Answering the pulses of thy sane and equable
heart,
Tuning a verse for thee.

O earth that hast no voice, confide to me a voice,
O harvest of my lands—O boundless summer growths,
O lavish brown parturient earth—O infinite teeming
womb,
A song to narrate thee.

2

Ever upon this stage,
Is acted God's calm annual drama,
Gorgeous processions, songs of birds,
Sunrise that fullest feeds and freshens most the soul,
The heaving sea, the waves upon the shore, the
musical, strong waves,
The woods, the stalwart trees, the slender, tapering
trees,
The liliput countless armies of the grass,
The heat, the showers, the measureless pasturages,

The scenery of the snows, the winds' free orchestra,
The stretching light-hung roof of clouds, the clear cerulean and the silvery fringes,
The high-dilating stars, the placid beckoning stars,
The moving flocks and herds, the plains and emerald meadows,
The shows of all the varied lands and all the growths and products.

3

Fecund America—to-day,
Thou art all over set in births and joys!
Thou groan'st with riches, thy wealth clothes thee as a swathing garment,
Thou laughest loud with ache of great possessions,
A myriad-twining life like interlacing vines binds all thy vast demesne,
As some huge ship freighted to water's edge thou ridest into port,
As rain falls from the heaven and vapours rise from the earth, so have the precious values fallen upon thee and risen out of thee;
Thou envy of the globe! thou miracle!
Thou, bathed, choked, swimming in plenty,
Thou lucky Mistress of the tranquil barns,
Thou Prairie Dame that sittest in the middle and lookest out upon thy world, and lookest East and lookest West,

Dispensatress, that by a word givest a thousand
miles, a million farms, and missest nothing,
Thou all-acceptress—thou hospitable (thou only
art hospitable as God is hospitable).

4

When late I sang sad was my voice,
Sad were the shows around me with deafening noises
of hatred and smoke of war;
In the midst of the conflict, the heroes, I stood,
Or pass'd with slow step through the wounded and
dying.

But now I sing not war,
Nor the measur'd march of soldiers, nor the tents of
camps,
Nor the regiments hastily coming up deploying in
line of battle;
No more the sad, unnatural shows of war.

Ask'd room those flush'd immortal ranks, the first
forth-stepping armies?
Ask room alas the ghastly ranks, the armies dread
that follow'd.

(Pass, pass, ye proud brigades, with your tramping
sinewy legs,
With your shoulders young and strong, with your
knapsacks and your muskets;

How elate I stood and watch'd you, where starting off you march'd.

Pass—then rattle drums again,
For an army heaves in sight, O another gathering army,
Swarming, trailing on the rear, O you dread accruing army,
O you regiments so piteous, with your mortal diarrhœa, with your fever,
O my land's maim'd darlings, with the plenteous bloody bandage and the crutch,
Lo, your pallid army follows.)

5

But on these days of brightness,
On the far-stretching beauteous landscape, the roads and lanes, the high-piled farm-wagons, and the fruits and barns,
Should the dead intrude?

Ah the dead to me mar not, they fit well in Nature,
They fit very well in the landscape under the trees and grass,
And along the edge of the sky in the horizon's far margin.

Nor do I forget you Departed,
Nor in winter or summer my lost ones,

But most in the open air as now when my soul is
rapt and at peace, like pleasing phantoms,
Your memories rising glide silently by me.

6

I saw the day the return of the heroes,
(Yet the heroes never surpass'd shall never return,
Them that day I saw not).

I saw the interminable corps, I saw the processions
of armies,
I saw them approaching, defiling by with divisions,
Streaming northward, their work done, camping
awhile in clusters of mighty camps.

No holiday soldiers—youthful, yet veterans,
Worn, swart, handsome, strong, of the stock of
homestead and workshop,
Harden'd of many a long campaign and sweaty
march,
Inured on many a hard-fought bloody field.

A pause—the armies wait,
A million flush'd embattled conquerors wait,
The world too waits, then soft as breaking night and
sure as dawn,
They melt, they disappear.

Exult O lands! victorious lands!
Not there your victory on those red shuddering fields,
But here and hence your victory.

Melt, melt away ye armies—disperse ye blue-clad soldiers,
Resolve ye back again, give up for good your deadly arms,
Other the arms the fields henceforth for you, or South or North,
With saner wars, sweet wars, life-giving wars.

7

Loud O my throat, and clear O soul!
The season of thanks and the voice of full-yielding,
The chant of joy and power for boundless fertility.

All till'd and untill'd fields expand before me,
I see the true arenas of my race, or first or last,
Man's innocent and strong arenas.

I see the heroes at other toils,
I see well-wielded in their hands the better weapons.

I see where the Mother of All,
With full-spanning eye gazes forth, dwells long,
And counts the varied gathering of the products.

Busy the far, the sunlit panorama,

Prairie, orchard, and yellow grain of the North,
Cotton and rice of the South and Louisianian cane,
Open unseeded fallows, rich fields of clover and timothy,
Kine and horses feeding, and droves of sheep and swine,
And many a stately river flowing and many a jocund brook,
And healthy uplands with herby-perfumed breezes,
And the good green grass, that delicate miracle the ever-recurring grass.

Toil on heroes! harvest the products!
Not alone on those warlike fields the Mother of All,
With dilated form and lambent eyes watch'd you.

Toil on heroes! toil well! handle the weapons well!
The Mother of All, yet here as ever she watches you.

Well-pleased America thou beholdest,
Over the fields of the West those crawling monsters,
The human-divine inventions, the labour-saving implements;
Beholdest moving in every direction imbued as with life the revolving hay-rakes,
The steam-power reaping-machines and the horse-power machines,

The engines, thrashers of grain and cleaners of grain, well separating the straw, the nimble work of the patent pitchfork,
Beholdest the newer saw-mill, the southern cotton-gin, and the rice-cleanser.

Beneath thy look O Maternal,
With these and else and with their own strong hands the heroes harvest.

All gather and all harvest,
Yet but for thee O Powerful, not a scythe might swing as now in security,
Not a maize-stalk dangle as now its silken tassels in peace.

Under thee only they harvest, even but a wisp of hay under thy great face only,
Harvest the wheat of Ohio, Illinois, Wisconsin, every barbed spear under thee,
Harvest the maize of Missouri, Kentucky, Tennessee, each ear in its light-green sheath,
Gather the hay to its myriad mows in the odorous tranquil barns,
Oats to their bins, the white potato, the buckwheat of Michigan, to theirs;
Gather the cotton in Mississippi or Alabama, dig and hoard the golden the sweet potato of Georgia and the Carolinas,

Clip the wool of California or Pennsylvania,
Cut the flax in the Middle States, or hemp or tobacco
in the Borders,
Pick the pea and the bean, or pull apples from the
trees or bunches of grapes from the vines,
Or aught that ripens in all these States or North or
South,
Under the beaming sun and under thee.

MEMORIES OF PRESIDENT LINCOLN

WHEN LILACS LAST IN THE DOOR-YARD BLOOM'D

WHEN lilacs last in the dooryard bloom'd,
And the great star early droop'd in the western sky in the night,
I mourn'd, and yet shall mourn with ever-returning spring.

Ever-returning spring, trinity sure to me you bring,
Lilac blooming perennial and drooping star in the west,
And thought of him I love.

2

O powerful western fallen star!
O shades of night—O moody, tearful night!
O great star disappear'd—O the black murk that hides the star!
O cruel hands that hold me powerless—O helpless soul of me!
O harsh surrounding cloud that will not free my soul.

3

In the dooryard fronting an old farm-house near the white-wash'd palings,
Stands the lilac-bush tall-growing with heart-shaped leaves of rich green,
With many a pointed blossom rising delicate, with the perfume strong I love,
With every leaf a miracle—and from this bush in the door-yard,
With delicate-colour'd blossoms and heart-shaped leaves of rich green,
A sprig with its flower I break.

4

In the swamp in secluded recesses,
A shy and hidden bird is warbling a song.

Solitary the thrush,
The hermit withdrawn to himself, avoiding the settlements,
Sings by himself a song.

Song of the bleeding throat,
Death's outlet song of life (for well dear brother I know,
If thou wast not granted to sing thou would'st surely die).

5

Over the breast of the spring, the land, amid cities,
Amid lanes and through old woods, where lately
the violets peep'd from the ground, spotting
the gray débris,
Amid the grass in the fields each side of the lanes,
passing the endless grass,
Passing the yellow-spear'd wheat, every grain from
its shroud in the dark-brown fields uprisen,
Passing the apple-tree blows of white and pink in
the orchards,
Carrying a corpse to where it shall rest in the grave,
Night and day journeys a coffin.

6

Coffin that passes through lanes and streets,
Through day and night with the great cloud darken-
ing the land,
With the pomp of the inloop'd flags with the cities
draped in black,
With the show of the States themselves as of crape-
veil'd women standing,
With processions long and winding and the flambeaus
of the night,
With the countless torches lit, with the silent sea
of faces and the unbared heads,
With the waiting depot, the arriving coffin, and the
sombre faces,

With dirges through the night, with the thousand
voices rising strong and solemn,
With all the mournful voices of the dirges pour'd
around the coffin,
The dim-lit churches and the shuddering organs—
where amid these you journey,
With the tolling tolling bells' perpetual clang,
Here, coffin that slowly passes,
I give you my sprig of lilac.

7

(Nor for you, for one alone,
Blossoms and branches green to coffins all I bring,
For fresh as the morning, thus would I chant a song
for you O sane and sacred death.

All over bouquets of roses,
O death, I cover you over with roses and early lilies,
But mostly and now the lilac that blooms the first,
Copious I break, I break the sprigs from the bushes,
With loaded arms I come, pouring for you,
For you and the coffins all of you O death.)

8

O western orb sailing the heaven,
Now I know what you must have meant as a month
since I walk'd,
As I walk'd in silence the transparent shadowy
night,

As I saw you had something to tell as you bent to
me night after night,
As you dropp'd from the sky low down as if to my
side (while the other stars all look'd on),
As we wander'd together the solemn night (for some-
thing I know not what kept me from sleep),
As the night advanced, and I saw on the rim of the
west how full you were of woe,
As I stood on the rising ground in the breeze in the
cool transparent night,
As I watch'd where you pass'd and was lost in the
netherward black of the night,
As my soul in its trouble dissatisfied sank, as where
you sad orb,
Concluded, dropt in the night, and was gone.

9

Sing on there in the swamp,
O singer bashful and tender, I hear your notes, I
hear your call,
I hear, I come presently, I understand you,
But a moment I linger, for the lustrous star has
detain'd me,
The star my departing comrade holds and detains me.

10

O how shall I warble myself for the dead one there
I loved?

And how shall I deck my song for the large sweet
soul that has gone?
And what shall my perfume be for the grave of
him I love?

Sea-winds blown from east and west,
Blown from the Eastern sea and blown from the
Western sea, till there on the prairies meeting,
These and with these and the breath of my chant,
I'll perfume the grave of him I love.

11

O what shall I hang on the chamber walls?
And what shall the pictures be that I hang on the
walls,
To adorn the burial-house of him I love?

Pictures of growing spring and farms and homes,
With the Fourth-month eve at sundown, and the
gray smoke lucid and bright,
With floods of the yellow gold of the gorgeous,
indolent, sinking sun, burning, expanding the
air,
With the fresh sweet herbage under foot, and the
pale green leaves of the trees prolific,
In the distance the flowing glaze, the breast of the
river, with a wind-dapple here and there,
With ranging hills on the banks, with many a line
against the sky, and shadows,

And the city at hand with dwellings so dense, and stacks of chimneys,
And all the scenes of life and the workshops, and the workmen homeward returning.

12

Lo, body and soul—this land,
My own Manhattan with spires, and the sparkling and hurrying tides, and the ships,
The varied and ample land, the South and the North in the light, Ohio's shores and flashing Missouri,
And ever the far-spreading prairies cover'd with grass and corn.

Lo, the most excellent sun so calm and haughty,
The violet and purple morn with just-felt breezes,
The gentle soft-born measureless light,
The miracle spreading bathing all, the fulfill'd noon,
The coming eve delicious, the welcome night and the stars,
Over my cities shining all, enveloping man and land.

13

Sing on, sing on you gray-brown bird,
Sing from the swamps, the recesses, pour your chant from the bushes,
Limitless out of the dusk, out of the cedars and pines.

Sing on dearest brother, warble your reedy song,
Loud human song, with voice of uttermost woe.

O liquid and free and tender!
O wild and loose to my soul—O wondrous singer!
You only I hear—yet the star holds me (but will
    soon depart),
Yet the lilac with mastering odour holds me.

14

Now while I sat in the day and look'd forth,
In the close of the day with its light and the fields of
    spring, and the farmers preparing their crops,
In the large unconscious scenery of my land with
    its lakes and forests,
In the heavenly aerial beauty (after the perturb'd
    winds and the storms),
Under the arching heavens of the afternoon swift
    passing, and the voices of children and women,
The many-moving sea-tides, and I saw the ships
    how they sail'd,
And the summer approaching with richness, and the
    fields all busy with labour,
And the infinite separate houses, how they all went
    on, each with its meals and minutia of daily
    usages,
And the streets how their throbbings throbb'd, and
    the cities pent—lo, then and there,

Falling upon them all and among them all, enveloping me with the rest,
Appear'd the cloud, appear'd the long black trail,
And I knew death, its thought, and the sacred knowledge of death.

Then with the knowledge of death as walking one side of me,
And the thought of death close-walking the other side of me,
And I in the middle as with companions, and as holding the hands of companions,
I fled forth to the hiding receiving night that talks not,
Down to the shores of the water, the path by the swamp in the dimness,
To the solemn shadowy cedars and ghostly pines so still.

And the singer so shy to the rest receiv'd me,
The gray-brown bird I know receiv'd us comrades three,
And he sang the carol of death, and a verse for him I love.

From deep secluded recesses,
From the fragrant cedars and the ghostly pines so still,
Came the carol of the bird.

And the charm of the carol rapt me,
As I held as if by their hands my comrades in the night,
And the voice of my spirit tallied the song of the bird.

Come lovely and soothing death,
Undulate round the world, serenely arriving, arriving,
In the day, in the night, to all, to each,
Sooner or later delicate death.

Prais'd be the fathomless universe,
For life and joy, and for objects and knowledge curious,
And for love, sweet love—but praise! praise! praise!
For the sure-enwinding arms of cool-enfolding death.

Dark mother always gliding near with soft feet,
Have none chanted for thee a chant of fullest welcome?
Then I chant it for thee, I glorify thee above all,
I bring thee a song that when thou must indeed come, come unfalteringly.

Approach strong deliveress,
When it is so, when thou hast taken them I joyously sing the dead,
Lost in the loving floating ocean of thee,
Laved in the flood of thy bliss O death.

From me to thee glad serenades,
Dances for thee I propose saluting thee, adornments and feastings for thee,
And the sights of the open landscape and the high-spread sky are fitting,
And life and the fields, and the huge and thoughtful night.

The night in silence under many a star,
The ocean shore and the husky whispering wave whose voice I know,
And the soul turning to thee O vast and well-veil'd death,
And the body gratefully nestling close to thee.

Over the tree-tops I float thee a song,
Over the rising and sinking waves, over the myriad fields and the prairies wide,
Over the dense-pack'd cities all and the teeming wharves and ways,
I float this carol with joy, with joy to thee O death.

15

To the tally of my soul,
Loud and strong kept up the gray-brown bird,
With pure deliberate notes spreading filling the night.

Loud in the pines and cedars dim,
Clear in the freshness moist and the swamp-perfume,
And I with my comrades there in the night.

While my sight that was bound in my eyes unclosed,
As to long panoramas of visions.

And I saw askant the armies,
I saw as in noiseless dreams hundreds of battle-flags,
Borne through the smoke of the battles and pierc'd with missiles I saw them,
And carried hither and yon through the smoke, and torn and bloody,
And at last but a few shreds left on the staffs (and all in silence),
And the staffs all splinter'd and broken.

I saw battle-corpses, myriads of them,
And the white skeletons of young men, I saw them,
I saw the débris and débris of all the slain soldiers of the war,
But I saw they were not as was thought,
They themselves were fully at rest, they suffer'd not,
The living remain'd and suffer'd, the mother suffer'd,
And the wife and the child and the musing comrade suffer'd,
And the armies that remain'd suffer'd.

16

Passing the visions, passing the night,
Passing, unloosing the hold of my comrades' hands,
Passing the song of the hermit bird and the tallying
song of my soul,
Victorious song, death's outlet song, yet varying
ever-altering song,
As low and wailing, yet clear the notes, rising and
falling, flooding the night,
Sadly sinking and fainting, as warning and warning,
and yet again bursting with joy,
Covering the earth and filling the spread of the
heaven,
As that powerful psalm in the night I heard from
recesses,
Passing, I leave thee lilac with heart-shaped leaves,
I leave thee there in the dooryard, blooming, return-
ing with spring.

I cease from my song for thee,
From my gaze on thee in the west, fronting the
west, communing with thee,
O comrade lustrous with silver face in the night.

Yet each to keep and all, retrievements out of the
night,
The song, the wondrous chant of the gray-brown
bird,

And the tallying chant, the echo arous'd in my soul,
With the lustrous and drooping star with the countenance full of woe,
With the holders holding my hand nearing the call of the bird,
Comrades mine and I in the midst, and their memory ever to keep, for the dead I loved so well,
For the sweetest, wisest soul of all my days and lands—and this for his dear sake,
Lilac and star and bird twined with the chant of my soul,
There in the fragrant pines and the cedars dusk and dim.

O CAPTAIN! MY CAPTAIN!

O CAPTAIN! my Captain! our fearful trip is done,
The ship has weather'd every rack, the prize we sought is won,
The port is near, the bells I hear, the people all exulting,
While follow eyes the steady keel, the vessel grim and daring;
But O heart! heart! heart!
O the bleeding drops of red,
Where on the deck my Captain lies,
Fallen cold and dead.

O Captain! my Captain! rise up and hear the bells;
Rise up—for you the flag is flung—for you the bugle trills,
For you bouquets and ribbon'd wreaths—for you the shores a-crowding,
For you they call, the swaying mass, their eager faces turning;
Here Captain! dear father!
This arm beneath your head!
It is some dream that on the deck,
You've fallen cold and dead.

My Captain does not answer, his lips are pale and still,
My father does not feel my arm, he has no pulse nor will,

The ship is anchor'd safe and sound, its voyage closed and done,
From fearful trip the victor ship comes in with object won;
Exult O shores, and ring O bells!
But I with mournful tread,
Walk the deck my Captain lies,
Fallen cold and dead.

HUSH'D BE THE CAMPS TO-DAY

(*May 4, 1865*)

Hush'd be the camps to-day,
And soldiers let us drape our war-worn weapons,
And each with musing soul retire to celebrate,
Our dear commander's death.

No more for him life's stormy conflicts,
Nor victory, nor defeat—no more time's dark events,
Charging like ceaseless clouds across the sky.

But sing poet in our name,
Sing of the love we bore him—because you, dweller
in camps, know it truly.

As they invault the coffin there,
Sing—as they close the doors of earth upon him—one
verse,
For the heavy hearts of soldiers.

Walt Whitman

ASHES OF SOLDIERS

Ashes of soldiers South or North,
As I muse retrospective murmuring a chant in thought,
The war resumes, again to my sense your shapes,
And again the advance of the armies.

Noiseless as mists and vapours,
From their graves in the trenches ascending,
From cemeteries all through Virginia and Tennessee,
From every point of the compass out of the countless graves,
In wafted clouds, in myriads large, or squads of twos or threes or single ones they come,
And silently gather round me.

Now sound no note O trumpeters,
Not at the head of my cavalry parading on spirited horses,
With sabres drawn and glistening, and carbines by their thighs (ah my brave horsemen!
My handsome tan-faced horsemen! what life, what joy and pride,
With all the perils were yours).

Nor you drummers, neither at reveillé at dawn,
Nor the long roll alarming the camp, nor even the
muffled beat for a burial,
Nothing from you this time O drummers bearing
my warlike drums.

But aside from these and the marts of wealth and the
crowded promenade,
Admitting around me comrades close unseen by the
rest and voiceless,
The slain elate and alive again, the dust and débris
alive,
I chant this chant of my silent soul in the name of all
dead soldiers.

Faces so pale with wondrous eyes, very dear, gather
closer yet,
Draw close, but speak not.

Phantoms of countless lost,
Invisible to the rest henceforth become my com-
panions,
Follow me ever—desert me not while I live.

Sweet are the blooming cheeks of the living—sweet
are the musical voices sounding,
But sweet, ah sweet, are the dead with their silent
eyes.

Walt Whitman

Dearest comrades, all is over and long gone,
But love is not over—and what love, O comrades!
Perfume from battlefields rising, up from the fœtor
arising.

Perfume therefore my chant, O love, immortal love,
Give me to bathe the memories of all dead soldiers,
Shroud them, embalm them, cover them all over
with tender pride.

Perfume all—make all wholesome,
Make these ashes to nourish and blossom,
O love, solve all, fructify all with the last chemistry.

Give me exhaustless, make me a fountain,
That I exhale love from me wherever I go like a
moist perennial dew,
For the ashes of all dead soldiers South or North.

PENSIVE ON HER DEAD GAZING

PENSIVE on her dead gazing I heard the Mother of All,
Desperate on the torn bodies, on the forms covering
the battlefields gazing
(As the last gun ceased, but the scent of the powder-
smoke linger'd),
As she call'd to her earth with mournful voice while
she stalk'd,
Absorb them well O my earth, she cried, I charge
you lose not my sons, lose not an atom,
And you streams absorb them well, taking their dear
blood,
And you local spots, and you airs that swim above
lightly impalpable,
And all you essences of soil and growth, and you my
rivers' depths,
And you mountain sides, and the woods where my
dear children's blood trickling redden'd,
And you trees down in your roots to bequeath to all
future trees,
My dead absorb or South or North—my young men's
bodies absorb, and their precious, precious
blood,
Which holding in trust for me faithfully back again
give me many a year hence,
In unseen essence and odour of surface and grass,
centuries hence,

In blowing airs from the fields back again give me
 my darlings, give my immortal heroes,
Exhale me them centuries hence, breathe me their
 breath, let not an atom be lost,
O years and graves! O air and soil! O my dead,
 an aroma sweet!
Exhale them perennial sweet death, years centuries
 hence.

III

POEMS OF AMERICA

I HEAR AMERICA SINGING

I HEAR America singing, the varied carols I hear,
Those of mechanics, each one singing his as it should be blithe and strong,
The carpenter singing his as he measures his plank or beam,
The mason singing his as he makes ready for work, or leaves off work,
The boatman singing what belongs to him in his boat, the deckhand singing on the steamboat deck,
The shoemaker singing as he sits on his bench, the hatter singing as he stands,
The wood-cutter's song, the ploughboy's on his way in the morning, or at noon intermission or at sundown,
The delicious singing of the mother, or of the young wife at work, or of the girl sewing or washing,
Each singing what belongs to him or her and to none else,
The day what belongs to the day—at night the party of young fellows, robust, friendly,
Singing with open mouths their strong melodious songs.

PIONEERS! O PIONEERS!

Come my tan-faced children,
Follow well in order, get your weapons ready,
Have you your pistols? have you your sharp-edged axes?
Pioneers! O pioneers!

For we cannot tarry here,
We must march my darlings, we must bear the brunt of danger
We the youthful sinewy races, all the rest on us depend,
Pioneers! O pioneers!

O you youths, Western youths,
So impatient, full of action, full of manly pride and friendship,
Plain I see you Western youths, see you tramping with the foremost,
Pioneers! O pioneers!

Have the elder races halted?
Do they droop and end their lesson, wearied over there beyond the seas?
We take up the task eternal, and the burden and the lesson,
Pioneers! O pioneers!

Walt Whitman

All the past we leave behind,
We debouch upon a newer mightier world, varied world,
Fresh and strong the world we seize, world of labour and the march,
Pioneers! O pioneers!

We detachments steady throwing,
Down the edges, through the passes, up the mountains steep,
Conquering, holding, daring, venturing as we go the unknown ways,
Pioneers! O pioneers!

We primeval forests felling,
We the rivers stemming, vexing we and piercing deep the mines within,
We the surface broad surveying, we the virgin soil upheaving,
Pioneers! O pioneers!

Colorado men are we,
From the peaks gigantic, from the great sierras and the high plateaus,
From the mine and from the gully, from the hunting trail we come,
Pioneers! O pioneers!

From Nebraska, from Arkansas,
Central inland race are we, from Missouri, with the continental blood intervein'd,
All the hands of comrades clasping, all the Southern, all the Northern,
Pioneers! O pioneers!

O resistless restless race!
O beloved race in all! O my breast aches with tender love for all!
O I mourn and yet exult, I am rapt with love for all,
Pioneers! O pioneers!

Raise the mighty mother mistress,
Waving high the delicate mistress, over all the starry mistress (bend your heads all),
Raise the fang'd and warlike mistress, stern, impassive, weapon'd mistress,
Pioneers! O pioneers!

See my children, resolute children,
By those swarms upon our rear we must never yield or falter,
Ages back in ghostly millions frowning there behind us urging,
Pioneers! O pioneers!

On and on the compact ranks,
With accessions ever waiting, with the places of the dead quickly fill'd,
Through the battle, through defeat, moving yet and never stopping,
Pioneers! O pioneers!

O to die advancing on!
Are there some of us to droop and die? has the hour come?
Then upon the march we fittest die, soon and sure the gap is fill'd,
Pioneers! O pioneers!

All the pulses of the world,
Falling in they beat for us, with the Western movement beat,
Holding single or together, steady moving to the front, all for us,
Pioneers! O pioneers!

Life's involv'd and varied pageants,
All the forms and shows, all the workmen at their work,
All the seamen and the landsmen, all the masters with their slaves,
Pioneers! O pioneers!

All the hapless silent lovers,
All the prisoners in the prisons, all the righteous and the wicked,
All the joyous, all the sorrowing, all the living, all the dying,
Pioneers! O pioneers!

I too with my soul and body,
We, a curious trio, picking, wandering on our way,
Through these shores amid the shadows, with the apparitions pressing,
Pioneers! O pioneers!

Lo, the darting bowling orb!
Lo, the brother orbs around, all the clustering sun and planets,
All the dazzling days, all the mystic nights with dreams,
Pioneers! O pioneers!

These are of us, they are with us,
All for primal needed work, while the followers there in embryo wait behind,
We to-day's procession heading, we the route for travel clearing,
Pioneers! O pioneers!

O you daughters of the West!
O you young and elder daughters! O you mothers and you wives!
Never must you be divided, in our ranks you move united,
Pioneers! O pioneers!

Minstrels latent on the prairies!
(Shrouded bards of other lands, you may rest, you have done your work)
Soon I hear you coming warbling, soon you rise and tramp amid us,
Pioneers! O pioneers!

Not for delectations sweet,
Not the cushion and the slipper, not the peaceful and the studious
Not the riches safe and palling, not for us the tame enjoyment,
Pioneers! O pioneers!

Do the feasters gluttonous feast?
Do the corpulent sleepers sleep? have they lock'd and bolted doors?
Still be ours the diet hard, and the blanket on the ground,
Pioneers! O pioneers!

Has the night descended?
Was the road of late so toilsome? did we stop discouraged nodding on our way?
Yet a passing hour I yield you in your tracks to pause oblivious,
Pioneers! O pioneers!

Till with sound of trumpet,
Far, far off the daybreak call—hark! how loud and clear I hear it wind,
Swift! to the head of the army!—swift! spring to your places,
Pioneers! O pioneers!

Walt Whitman

SONG OF THE BROAD-AXE

1

WEAPON shapely, naked, wan,
Head from the mother's bowels drawn,
Wooded flesh and metal bone, limb only one and lip only one,
Gray-blue leaf by red-heat grown, helve produced from a little seed sown
Resting the grass amid and upon,
To be lean'd and to lean on.

Strong shapes and attributes of strong shapes, masculine trades, sights and sounds,
Long varied train of an emblem, dabs of music,
Fingers of the organist skipping staccato over the keys of the great organ.

2

Welcome are all earth's lands, each for its kind,
Welcome are lands of pine and oak,
Welcome are lands of the lemon and fig,
Welcome are lands of gold,
Welcome are lands of wheat and maize, welcome those of the grape,
Welcome are lands of sugar and rice,

Welcome the cotton-lands, welcome those of the white potato and sweet potato,
Welcome are mountains, flats, sands, forests, prairies,
Welcome the rich borders of rivers, table-lands, openings,
Welcome the measureless grazing-lands, welcome the teeming soil of orchards, flax, honey, hemp;
Welcome just as much the other more hard-faced lands,
Lands rich as lands of gold or wheat and fruit lands,
Lands of mines, lands of the manly and rugged ores,
Lands of coal, copper, lead, tin, zinc,
Lands of iron—lands of the make of the axe.

3

The log at the wood-pile, the axe supported by it,
The sylvan hut, the vine over the doorway, the space clear'd for a garden,
The irregular tapping of rain down on the leaves after the storm is lull'd,
The wailing and moaning at intervals, the thought of the sea,
The thought of ships struck in the storm and put on their beam ends, and the cutting away of masts,
The sentiment of the huge timbers of old-fashion'd houses and barns,

The remember'd print or narrative, the voyage at a
venture of men, families, goods,
The disembarkation, the founding of a new city,
The voyage of those who sought a New England
and found it, the outset anywhere,
The settlements of the Arkansas, Colorado, Ottawa,
Willamette,
The slow progress, the scant fare, the axe, rifle,
saddle-bags;
The beauty of all adventurous and daring persons,
The beauty of wood-boys and wood-men with their
clear untrimm'd faces,
The beauty of independence, departure, actions
that rely on themselves,
The American contempt for statutes and ceremonies,
the boundless impatience of restraint,
The loose drift of character, the inkling through random types, the solidification;
The butcher in the slaughter-house, the hands
aboard schooners and sloops, the raftsman,
the pioneer,
Lumbermen in their winter camp, daybreak in the
woods, stripes of snow on the limbs of trees,
the occasional snapping,
The glad clear sound of one's own voice, the merry
song, the natural life of the woods, the strong
day's work,

The blazing fire at night, the sweet taste of supper, the talk, the bed of hemlock-boughs, and the bear-skin;
The house-builder at work in cities or anywhere,
The preparatory jointing, squaring, sawing, mortising,
The hoist-up of beams, the push of them in their places, laying them regular,
Setting the studs by their tenons in the mortises according as they were prepared,
The blows of mallets and hammers, the attitudes of the men, their curv'd limbs,
Bending, standing, astride the beams, driving in pins, holding on by posts and braces,
The hook'd arm over the plate, the other arm wielding the axe,
The floor-men forcing the planks close to be nail'd,
Their postures bringing their weapons downward on the bearers,
The echoes resounding through the vacant building;
The huge storehouse carried up in the city well under way,
The six framing-men, two in the middle and two at each end, carefully bearing on their shoulders a heavy stick for a cross-beam,
The crowded line of masons with trowels in their right hands rapidly laying the long side-wall, two hundred feet from front to rear,

The flexible rise and fall of backs, the continual click of the trowels striking the bricks,
The bricks one after another each laid so workmanlike in its place, and set with a knock of the trowel-handle,
The piles of materials, the mortar on the mortar-boards, and the steady replenishing by the hod-men;
Spar-makers in the spar-yard, the swarming row of well-grown apprentices,
The swing of their axes on the square-hew'd log shaping it toward the shape of a mast,
The brisk short crackle of the steel driven slantingly into the pine,
The butter-colour'd chips flying off in great flakes and slivers,
The limber motion of brawny young arms and hips in easy costumes,
The constructor of wharves, bridges, piers, bulk-heads, floats, stays against the sea;
The city fireman, the fire that suddenly bursts forth in the close-pack'd square,
The arriving engines, the hoarse shouts, the nimble stepping and daring,
The strong command through the fire-trumpets, the falling in line, the rise and fall of the arms forcing the water,

The slender, spasmic, blue-white jets, the bringing
to bear of the hooks and ladders and their
execution,
The crash and cut away of connecting wood-work, or
through floors if the fire smoulders under them,
The crowd with their lit faces watching, the glare
and dense shadows;
The forger at his forge-furnace and the user of iron
after him,
The maker of the axe large and small, and the welder
and temperer,
The chooser breathing his breath on the cold steel
and trying the edge with his thumb,
The one who clean-shapes the handle and sets it
firmly in the socket;
The shadowy processions of the portraits of the past
users also,
The primal patient mechanics, the architects and
engineers,
The far-off Assyrian edifice and Mizra edifice,
The Roman lictors preceding the consuls,
The antique European warrior with his axe in com-
bat,
The uplifted arm, the clatter of blows on the hel-
meted head,
The death-howl, the limpsy tumbling body, the
rush of friend and foe thither,
The siege of revolted lieges determin'd for liberty,

The summons to surrender, the battering at castle
 gates, the truce and parley,
The sack of an old city in its time.
The bursting in of mercenaries and bigots tumultu-
 ously and disorderly,
Roar, flames, blood, drunkenness, madness,
Goods freely rifled from houses and temples, screams
 of women in the gripe of brigands,
Craft and thievery of camp-followers, men running,
 old persons despairing,
The hell of war, the cruelties of creeds,
The list of all executive deeds and words just or
 unjust,
The power of personality just or unjust.

4

Muscle and pluck forever!
What invigorates life invigorates death,
And the dead advance as much as the living advance,
And the future is no more uncertain than the present,
For the roughness of the earth and of man encloses
 as much as the delicatesse of the earth and of
 man,
And nothing endures but personal qualities.

What do you think endures?
Do you think a great city endures?
Or a teeming manufacturing state? or a prepared
 constitution? or the best built steamships?

Or hotels of granite and iron? or any chef-d'œuvres of engineering, forts, armaments?

Away! these are not to be cherish'd for themselves,
They fill their hour, the dancers dance, the musicians play for them,
The show passes, all does well enough of course,
All does very well till one flash of defiance.

A great city is that which has the greatest men and women,
If it be a few ragged huts it is still the greatest city in the whole world.

5

The place where a great city stands is not the place of stretch'd wharves, docks, manufactures, deposits of produce merely,
Nor the place of ceaseless salutes of new-comers or the anchor-lifters of the departing,
Nor the place of the tallest and costliest buildings or shops selling goods from the rest of the earth,
Nor the place of the best libraries and schools, nor the place where money is plentiest,
Nor the place of the most numerous population.

Where the city stands with the brawniest breed of orators and bards,

Where the city stands that is belov'd by these, and
loves them in return and understands them,
Where no monuments exist to heroes but in the common words and deeds,
Where thrift is in its place, and prudence is in its
place,
Where the men and women think lightly of the laws,
Where the slave ceases, and the master of slaves
ceases,
Where the populace rise at once against the never-ending audacity of elected persons,
Where fierce men and women pour forth as the sea
to the whistle of death pours its sweeping
and unript waves,
Where outside authority enters always after the
precedence of inside authority,
Where the citizen is always the head and ideal,
and President, Mayor, Governor and what
not, are agents for pay,
Where children are taught to be laws to themselves,
and to depend on themselves,
Where equanimity is illustrated in affairs,
Where speculations on the soul are encouraged,
Where women walk in public processions in the
streets the same as the men,
Where they enter the public assembly and take
places the same as the men;
Where the city of the faithfulest friends stands,

Where the city of the cleanliness of the sexes stands,
Where the city of the healthiest fathers stands,
Where the city of the best-bodied mothers stands,
There the great city stands.

6

How beggarly appear arguments before a defiant deed!
How the floridness of the materials of cities shrivels before a man's or woman's look!

All waits or goes by default till a strong being appears;
A strong being is the proof of the race and of the ability of the universe,
When he or she appears materials are overaw'd,
The dispute on the soul stops,
The old customs and phrases are confronted, turn'd back, or laid away.

What is your money-making now? what can it do now?
What is your respectability now?
What are your theology, tuition, society, traditions, statute-books, now?
Where are your jibes of being now?
Where are your cavils about the soul now?

7

A sterile landscape covers the ore, there is as good
as the best for all the forbidding appearance,
There is the mine, there are the miners,
The forge-furnace is there, the melt is accomplish'd,
the hammers-men are at hand with their
tongs and hammers,
What always served and always serves is at hand.

Than this nothing has better served, it has served
all,
Served the fluent-tongued and subtle-sensed Greek,
and long ere the Greek,
Served in building the buildings that last longer
than any,
Served the Hebrew, the Persian, the most ancient
Hindustanee,
Served the mound-raiser on the Mississippi, served
those whose relics remain in Central America,
Served Albic temples in woods or on plains, with
unhewn pillars and the druids,
Served the artificial clefts, vast, high, silent, on the
snow-cover'd hills of Scandinavia,
Served those who time out of mind made on the
granite walls rough sketches of the sun, moon,
stars, ships, ocean waves,
Served the paths of the irruptions of the Goths,
served the pastoral tribes and nomads,

Served the long distant Kelt, served the hardy pirates of the Baltic,
Served before any of those the venerable and harmless men of Ethiopia,
Served the making of helms for the galleys of pleasure and the making of those for war,
Served all great works on land and all great works on the sea,
For the mediæval ages and before the mediæval ages,
Served not the living only then as now, but served the dead.

8

I see the European headsman,
He stands mask'd, clothed in red, with huge legs and strong naked arms,
And leans on a ponderous axe.

(Whom have you slaughter'd lately European headsman?
Whose is that blood upon you so wet and sticky?)

I see the clear sunsets of the martyrs,
I see from the scaffolds the descending ghosts,
Ghosts of dead lords, uncrown'd ladies, impeach'd ministers, rejected kings,
Rivals, traitors, poisoners, disgraced chieftains and the rest.

I see those who in any land have died for the good
cause,
The seed is spare, nevertheless the crop shall never
run out
(Mind you O foreign kings, O priests, the crop shall
never run out).

I see the blood wash'd entirely away from the axe,
Both blade and helve are clean,
They spirt no more the blood of European nobles,
they clasp no more the necks of queens.

I see the headsman withdraw and become useless,
I see the scaffold untrodden and mouldy, I see no
longer any axe upon it,
I see the mighty and friendly emblem of the power
of my own race, the newest, largest race.

9

(America! I do not vaunt my love for you,
I have what I have.)

The axe leaps!
The solid forest gives fluid utterances,
They tumble forth, they rise and form,
Hut, tent, landing, survey,
Flail, plough, pick, crowbar, spade,

Shingle, rail, prop, wainscot, jamb, lath, panel, gable,
Citadel, ceiling, saloon, academy, organ, exhibition-house, library,
Cornice, trellis, pilaster, balcony, window, turret, porch,
Hoe, rake, pitchfork, pencil, wagon, staff, saw, jack-plane, mallet, wedge, rounce,
Chair, tub, hoop, table, wicket, vane, sash, floor,
Work-box, chest, string'd instrument, boat frame, and what not,
Capitols of States, and capitol of the nation of States,
Long stately rows in avenues, hospitals for orphans or for the poor or sick,
Manhattan steamboats and clippers taking the measure of all seas.

The shapes arise!
Shapes of the using of axes anyhow, and the users and all that neighbours them,
Cutters down of wood and haulers of it to the Penobscot or Kennebec,
Dwellers in cabins among the Californian mountains or by the little lakes, or on the Columbia,
Dwellers south on the banks of the Gila or Rio Grande, friendly gatherings, the characters and fun,
Dwellers along the St. Lawrence, or north in Kanada, or down by the Yellowstone, dwellers on coasts and off coasts,

Seal-fishers, whalers, arctic seamen breaking passages through the ice.

The shapes arise!
Shapes of factories, arsenals, foundries, markets,
Shapes of the two-threaded tracks of railroads,
Shapes of the sleepers of bridges, vast frameworks, girders, arches,
Shapes of the fleets of barges, tows, lake and canal craft, river craft,
Ship-yards and dry-docks along the Eastern and Western seas, and in many a bay and by-place,
The live-oak kelsons, the pine planks, the spars, the hackmatack-roots for knees,
The ships themselves on their ways, the tiers of scaffolds, the workmen busy outside and inside,
The tools lying around, the great auger and little auger, the adze, bolt, line, square, gouge, and bead-plane.

10

The shapes arise!
The shape measur'd, saw'd, jack'd, join'd, stain'd,
The coffin-shape for the dead to lie within in his shroud,

The shape got out in posts, in the bedstead posts,
in the posts of the bride's bed,
The shape of the little trough, the shape of the
rockers beneath, the shape of the babe's
cradle,
The shape of the floor-planks, the floor-planks for
dancers' feet,
The shape of the planks of the family home, the
home of the friendly parents and children,
The shape of the roof of the home of the happy
young man and woman, the roof over the
well-married young man and woman,
The roof over the supper joyously cook'd by the
chaste wife, and joyously eaten by the chaste
husband, content after his day's work.

The shapes arise!
The shape of the prisoner's place in the court-room,
and of him or her seated in the place,
The shape of the liquor-bar lean'd against by the
young rum-drinker and the old rum-drinker,
The shape of the shamed and angry stairs trod by
sneaking footsteps,
The shape of the sly settee, and the adulterous
unwholesome couple,
The shape of the gambling-board with its devilish
winnings and losings,

The shape of the step-ladder for the convicted and sentenced murderer, the murderer with haggard face and pinion'd arms,
The sheriff at hand with his deputies, the silent and white-lipp'd crowd, the dangling of the rope.

The shapes arise!
Shapes of doors giving many exits and entrances,
The door passing the dissever'd friend flush'd and in haste,
The door that admits good news and bad news,
The door whence the son left home confident and puff'd up,
The door he enter'd again from a long and scandalous absence, diseas'd, broken down, without innocence, without means.

11

Her shape arises,
She less guarded than ever, yet more guarded than ever,
The gross and soil'd she moves among do not make her gross and soil'd,
She knows the thoughts as she passes, nothing is conceal'd from her,
She is none the less considerate or friendly therefor,

She is the best belov'd, it is without exception, she has no reason to fear and she does not fear,
Oaths, quarrels, hiccupp'd songs, smutty expressions, are idle to her as she passes,
She is silent, she is possess'd of herself, they do not offend her,
She receives them as the laws of Nature receive them, she is strong,
She too is a law of Nature—there is no law stronger than she is.

12

The main shapes arise!
Shapes of Democracy total, result of centuries,
Shapes ever projecting other shapes,
Shapes of turbulent manly cities,
Shapes of the friends and home-givers of the whole earth,
Shapes bracing the earth and braced with the whole earth.

Walt Whitman

GIVE ME THE SPLENDID SILENT SUN

1

GIVE me the splendid silent sun with all his beams full-dazzling,
Give me juicy autumnal fruit ripe and red from the orchard,
Give me a field where the unmow'd grass grows,
Give me an arbour, give me the trellis'd grape,
Give me fresh corn and wheat, give me serene-moving animals teaching content,
Give me nights perfectly quiet as on high plateaus west of the Mississippi, and I looking up at the stars,
Give me odorous at sunrise a garden of beautiful flowers where I can walk undisturb'd,
Give me for marriage a sweet-breath'd woman of whom I should never tire,
Give me a perfect child, give me away aside from the noise of the world a rural domestic life,
Give me to warble spontaneous songs recluse by myself, for my own ears only,
Give me solitude, give me Nature, give me again O Nature your primal sanities!

These demanding to have them (tired with ceaseless excitement, and rack'd by the war-strife),

These to procure incessantly asking, rising in cries
from my heart,
While yet incessantly asking still I adhere to my city,
Day upon day and year upon year O city, walking
your streets,
Where you hold me enchain'd a certain time refusing
to give me up,
Yet giving to make me glutted, enrich'd of soul,
you give me forever faces
(O I see what I sought to escape, confronting, revers-
ing my cries,
I see my own soul trampling down what it ask'd
for).

2

Keep your splendid silent sun,
Keep your woods, O Nature, and the quiet places
by the woods,
Keep your fields of clover and timothy, and your
corn-fields and orchards,
Keep the blossoming buckwheat fields where the
Ninth-month bees hum;
Give me faces and streets—give me these phantoms
incessant and endless along the trottoirs!
Give me interminable eyes—give me women—give
me comrades and lovers by the thousand!
Let me see new ones every day—let me hold new
ones by the hand every day!

Give me such shows—give me the streets of Manhattan!
Give me Broadway, with the soldiers marching—give me the sound of the trumpets and drums!
(The soldiers in companies or regiments—some starting away, flushed and reckless,
Some, their time up, returning with thinn'd ranks, young, yet very old, worn, marching, noticing nothing)
Give me the shores and wharves heavy-fringed with black ships!
O such for me! O an intense life, full to repletion and varied!
The life of the theatre, bar-room, huge hotel, for me!
The saloon of the steamer! the crowded excursion for me! the torchlight procession!
The dense brigade bound for the war, with high piled military wagons following;
People, endless, streaming, with strong voices, passions, pageants,
Manhattan streets with their powerful throbs, with beating drums as now,
The endless and noisy chorus, the rustle and clank of muskets (even the sight of the wounded),
Manhattan crowds, with their turbulent musical chorus!
Manhattan faces and eyes forever for me.

FACES

The old face of the mother of many children,
Whist! I am fully content.

Lull'd and late is the smoke of the First-day morning,
It hangs low over the rows of trees by the fences,
It hangs thin by the sassafras and wild-cherry and cat-brier under them.

I saw the rich ladies in full dress at the soiree,
I heard what the singers were singing so long,
Heard who sprang in crimson youth from the white froth and the water-blue.

Behold a woman!
She looks out from her quaker cap, her face is clearer and more beautiful than the sky.

She sits in an armchair under the shaded porch of the farmhouse,
The sun just shines on her old white head.

Her ample gown is of cream-hued linen,
Her grandsons raised the flax, and her granddaughters spun it with the distaff and the wheel.

Walt Whitman

The melodious character of the earth,
The finish beyond which philosophy cannot go and
does not wish to go,
The justified mother of men.

O MAGNET-SOUTH

O MAGNET-SOUTH! O glistening perfumed South! my South!
O quick mettle, rich blood, impulse and love! good and evil! O all dear to me!
O dear to me my birth-things—all moving things and the trees where I was born—the grains, plants, rivers,
Dear to me my own slow sluggish rivers where they flow, distant, over flats of silvery sands or through swamps,
Dear to me the Roanoke, the Savannah, the Altamahaw, the Pedee, the Tombigbee, the Santee, the Coosa, and the Sabine,
O pensive, far away wandering, I return with my soul to haunt their banks again,
Again in Florida I float on transparent lakes, I float on the Okeechobee, I cross the hummock-land or through pleasant openings or dense forests,
I see the parrots in the woods, I see the papaw-tree and the blossoming titi;
Again, sailing in my coaster on deck, I coast off Georgia, I coast up the Carolinas,
I see where the live-oak is growing, I see where the yellow-pine, the scented bay-tree, the lemon and orange, the cypress, the graceful palmetto,

I pass rude sea-headlands and enter Pamlico
sound through an inlet, and dart my vision
inland;
O the cotton plant! the growing fields of rice, sugar,
hemp!
The cactus guarded with thorns, the laurel-tree with
large white flowers,
The range afar, the richness and barrenness, the
old woods charged with mistletoe and trail-
ing moss,
The piney odour and the gloom, the awful natural
stillness (here in these dense swamps the
freebooter carries his gun, and the fugitive
has his conceal'd hut);
O the strange fascination of these half-known half-
impassable swamps, infested by reptiles, re-
sounding with the bellow of the alligator, the
sad noises of the night-owl and the wild-cat,
and the whirr of the rattlesnake,
The mocking-bird, the American mimic, singing all
the forenoon, singing through the moon-lit
night,
The humming-bird, the wild turkey, the raccoon,
the opossum;
A Kentucky corn-field, the tall, graceful, long-leav'd
corn, slender, flapping, bright green, with
tassels, with beautiful ears each well-sheath'd
in its husk;

O my heart! O tender and fierce pangs, I can stand
them not, I will depart;
O to be a Virginian where I grew up! O to be a
Carolinian!
O longings irrepressible! O I will go back to old
Tennessee and never wander more.

Walt Whitman

BY BROAD POTOMAC'S SHORE

By broad Potomac's shore, again old tongue
(Still uttering, still ejaculating, canst never cease
this babble?)
Again old heart so gay, again to you, your sense,
the full flush spring returning,
Again the freshness and the odours, again Virginia's
summer sky, pellucid blue and silver,
Again the forenoon purple of the hills,
Agagin the deathless grass, so noiseless soft and
green,
Again the blood-red roses blooming.

Perfume this book of mine O blood-red roses!
Lave subtly with your waters every line Potomac!
Give me of you O spring, before I close, to put be-
tween its pages!
O forenoon purple of the hills, before I close, of you!
O deathless grass, of you!

OUR OLD FEUILLAGE!

ALWAYS our old feuillage!
Always Florida's green peninsula—always the priceless delta of Louisiana—always the cotton-fields of Alabama and Texas,
Always California's golden hills and hollows, and the silver mountains of New Mexico—always soft-breath'd Cuba,
Always the vast slope drain'd by the Southern sea, inseparable with the slopes drain'd by the Eastern and Western seas,
The area the eighty-third year of these States, the three and a half millions of square miles,
The eighteen thousand miles of sea-coast and bay-coast on the main, the thirty thousand miles of river navigation,
The seven millions of distinct families and the same number of dwellings—always these, and more, branching forth into numberless branches,
Always the free range and diversity—always the continent of Democracy;
Always the prairies, pastures, forests, vast cities, travellers, Kanada, the snows;
Always these compact lands tied at the hips with the belt stringing the huge oval lakes;

Always the West with strong native persons, the increasing density there, the habitans, friendly, threatening, ironical, scorning invaders;
All sights, South, North, East—all deeds promiscuously done at all times,
All characters, movements, growths, a few noticed, myriads unnoticed,
Through Mannahatta's streets I walking, these things gathering,
On interior rivers by night in the glare of pine knots, steamboats wooding up,
Sunlight by day on the valley of the Susquehanna, and on the valleys of the Potomac and Rappahannock, and the valleys of the Roanoke and Delaware,
In their northerly wilds beasts of prey haunting the Adirondacks the hills, or lapping the Saginaw waters to drink,
In a lonesome inlet a sheldrake lost from the flock, sitting on the water rocking silently,
In farmers' barns oxen in the stable, their harvest labour done, they rest standing, they are too tired,
Afar on arctic ice the she-walrus lying drowsily while her cubs play around,
The hawk sailing where men have not yet sail'd, the farthest polar sea, ripply, crystalline, open, beyond the floes,

White drift spooning ahead where the ship in the tempest dashes,
On solid land what is done in cities as the bells strike midnight together,
In primitive woods the sounds there also sounding, the howl of the wolf, the scream of the panther, and the hoarse bellow of the elk,
In winter beneath the hard blue ice of Moosehead lake, in summer visible through the clear waters, the great trout swimming,
In lower latitudes in warmer air in the Carolinas the large black buzzard floating slowly high beyond the tree tops,
Below, the red cedar festoon'd with tylandria, the pines and cypresses growing out of the white sand that spreads far and flat,
Rude boats descending the big Pedee, climbing plants, parasites with colour'd flowers and berries enveloping huge trees,
The waving drapery on the live-oak trailing long and low, noiselessly waved by the wind,
The camp of Georgia wagoners just after dark, the supper-fires and the cooking and eating by whites and negroes,
Thirty or forty great wagons, the mules, cattle, horses, feeding from troughs,
The shadows, gleams, up under the leaves of the old sycamore-trees, the flames with the black

smoke from the pitch-pine curling and rising;
Southern fishermen fishing, the sounds and inlets of North Carolina's coast, the shad-fishery and the herring-fishery, the large sweep-seines, the windlasses on shore work'd by horses, the clearing, curing, and packing-houses;
Deep in the forest in piney woods turpentine dropping from the incisions in the trees, there are the turpentine works,
There are the negroes at work in good health, the ground in all directions is cover'd with pine straw;
In Tennessee and Kentucky slaves busy in the coalings, at the forge, by the furnace-blaze, or at the corn-shucking,
In Virginia, the planter's son returning after a long absence, joyfully welcom'd and kiss'd by the aged mulatto nurse,
On rivers boatmen safely moor'd at nightfall in their boats under shelter of high banks,
Some of the younger men dance to the sound of the banjo or fiddle, others sit on the gunwale smoking and talking;
Late in the afternoon the mocking-bird, the American mimic, singing in the Great Dismal Swamp,

There are the greenish waters, the resinous odour, the plenteous moss, the cypress-tree, and the juniper-tree;
Northward, young men of Mannahatta, the target company from an excursion returning home at evening, the musket-muzzles all bear bunches of flowers presented by women;
Children at play, or on his father's lap a young boy fallen asleep (how his lips move! how he smiles in his sleep!),
The scout riding on horseback over the plains west of the Mississippi, he ascends a knoll and sweeps his eyes around;
California life, the miner, bearded, dress'd in his rude costume, the stanch California friendship, the sweet air, the graves one in passing meets solitary just aside the horse-path;
Down in Texas the cotton-field, the negro-cabins, drivers driving mules or oxen before rude carts, cotton bales piled on banks and wharves;
Encircling all, vast-darting up and wide, the American Soul, with equal hemispheres, one Love, one Dilation or Pride;
In arrière the peace-talk with the Iroquois the aborigines, the calumet, the pipe of good-will, arbitration, and indorsement,
The sachem blowing the smoke first toward the sun and then toward the earth,

The drama of the scalp-dance enacted with painted
faces and guttural exclamations,
The setting out of the war-party, the long and
stealthy march,
The single file, the swinging hatchets, the surprise
and slaughter of enemies;
All the acts, scenes, ways, persons, attitudes of
these States, reminiscences, institutions,
All these States compact, every square mile of these
States without excepting a particle;
Me pleas'd, rambling in lanes and country fields,
Paumanok's fields,
Observing the spiral flight of two little yellow butter-
flies shuffling between each other, ascending
high in the air,
The darting swallow, the destroyer of insects, the
fall traveller southward but returning north-
ward early in the spring,
The country boy at the close of the day driving the
herd of cows and shouting to them as they
loiter to browse by the roadside,
The city wharf, Boston, Philadelphia, Baltimore,
Charleston, New Orleans, San Francisco,
The departing ships when the sailors heave at the
capstan;
Evening—me in my room—the setting sun,
The setting summer sun shining in my open window,
showing the swarm of flies, suspended, bal-

ancing in the air in the centre of the room, darting athwart, up and down, casting swift shadows in specks on the opposite wall where the shine is;
The athletic American matron speaking in public to crowds of listeners,
Males, females, immigrants, combinations, the copiousness, the individuality of the States, each for itself—the money-makers,
Factories, machinery, the mechanical forces, the windlass, lever, pulley, all certainties,
The certainty of space, increase, freedom, futurity,
In space the sporades, the scatter'd islands, the stars —on the firm earth, the lands, my lands,
O lands! all so dear to me—what you are (whatever it is), I putting it at random in these songs, become a part of that, whatever it is,
Southward there, I screaming, with wings slow flapping, with the myriads of gulls wintering along the coasts of Florida,
Otherways there atwixt the banks of the Arkansaw, the Rio Grande, the Nueces, the Brazos, the Tombigbee, the Red River, the Saskatchewan or the Osage, I with the spring waters laughing and skipping and running,
Northward, on the sands, on some shallow bay of Paumanok, I with parties of snowy herons wading in the wet to seek worms and aquatic plants,

Retreating, triumphantly twittering, the king-bird, from piercing the crow with its bill, for amusement—and I triumphantly twittering,
The migrating flock of wild geese alighting in autumn to refresh themselves, the body of the flock feed, the sentinels outside move around with erect heads watching, and are from time to time reliev'd by other sentinels—and I feeding and taking turns with the rest,
In Kanadian forests the moose, large as an ox, corner'd by hunters, rising desperately on his hind-feet, and plunging with his fore-feet, the hoofs as sharp as knives—and I, plunging at the hunters, corner'd and desperate,
In the Mannahatta, streets, piers, shipping, storehouses, and the countless workmen working in the shops,
And I too of the Mannahatta, singing thereof—and no less in myself than the whole of the Mannahatta in itself,
Singing the song of These, my ever-united lands—my body no more inevitable united, part to part, and made out of a thousand diverse contributions one identity, any more than my lands are inevitably united and made ONE IDENTITY;
Nativities, climates, the grass of the great pastoral Plains,

Cities, labours, death, animals, products, war, good and evil—these me,
These affording, in all their particulars, the old feuillage to me and to America, how can I do less than pass the clew of the union of them, to afford the like to you?
Whoever you are! how can I but offer you divine leaves, that you also be eligible as I am?
How can I but as here chanting, invite you for yourself to collect bouquets of the incomparable feuillage of these States?

Walt Whitman

A BROADWAY PAGEANT

I

OVER the Western sea hither from Niphon come,
Courteous, the swart-cheek'd two-sworded envoys,
Leaning back in their open barouches, bare-headed, impassive,
Ride to-day through Manhattan.

Libertad! I do not know whether others behold what I behold,
In the procession along with the nobles of Niphon, the errand-bearers,
Bringing up the rear, hovering above, around, or in the ranks marching,
But I will sing you a song of what I behold Libertad.

When million-footed Manhattan unpent descends to her pavements,
When the thunder-cracking guns arouse me with the proud roar I love,
When the round-mouth'd guns out of the smoke and smell I love spit their salutes,
When the fire-flashing guns have fully alerted me, and heaven-clouds canopy my city with a delicate thin haze,

When gorgeous the countless straight stems, the forests at the wharves, thicken with colours,
When every ship richly drest carries her flag at the peak,
When pennants trail and street-festoons hang from the windows,
When Broadway is entirely given up to foot-passengers and foot-standers, when the mass is densest,
When the façades of the houses are alive with people, when eyes gaze riveted tens of thousands at a time,
When the guests from the islands advance, when the pageant moves forward visible,
When the summons is made, when the answer that waited thousands of years answers,
I too arising, answering, descend to the pavements, merge with the crowd, and gaze with them.

2

Superb-faced Manhattan!
Comrade Americanos! to us, then at last the Orient comes.

To us, my city,
Where our tall-topt marble and iron beauties range on opposite sides, to walk in the space between,
To-day our Antipodes comes.

The Originatress comes,
The nest of languages, the bequeather of poems, the race of eld,
Florid with blood, pensive, rapt with musings, hot with passion,
Sultry with perfume, with ample and flowing garments,
With sunburnt visage, with intense soul and glittering eyes,
The race of Brahma comes.

See my cantabile! these and more are flashing to us from the procession,
As it moves changing, a kaleidoscope divine it moves changing before us.

For not the envoys nor the tann'd Japanee from his island only,
Lithe and silent the Hindoo appears, the Asiatic continent itself appears, the past, the dead,
The murky night-morning of wonder and fable inscrutable,
The envelop'd mysteries, the old and unknown hive-bees,
The north, the sweltering south, eastern Assyria, the Hebrews, the ancient of ancients,
Vast desolated cities, the gliding present, all of these and more are in the pageant-procession.

Geography, the world, is in it,
The Great Sea, the brood of islands, Polynesia, the coast beyond,
The coast you henceforth are facing—you Libertad! from your Western golden shores,
The countries there with their populations, the millions en-masse are curiously here,
The swarming market-places, the temples with idols ranged along the sides or at the end, bonze, brahmin, and llama,
Mandarin, farmer, merchant, mechanic, and fisherman,
The singing-girl and the dancing-girl, the ecstatic persons, the secluded emperors,
Confucius himself, the great poets and heroes, the warriors, the castes, all,
Trooping up, crowding from all directions, from the Altay mountains,
From Thibet, from the four winding and far-flowing rivers of China,
From the southern peninsulas and the demi-continental islands, from Malaysia,
These and whatever belongs to them palpable show forth to me, and are seiz'd by me,
And I am seiz'd by them, and friendlily held by them,
Till as here them all I chant, Libertad! for themselves and for you.

For I too raising my voice join the ranks of this pageant,
I am the chanter, I chant aloud over the pageant,
I chant the world on my Western sea,
I chant copious the islands beyond, thick as stars in the sky,
I chant the new empire grander than any before, as in a vision it comes to me,
I chant America the mistress, I chant a greater supremacy,
I chant projected a thousand blooming cities yet in time on those groups of sea-islands,
My sail-ships and steam-ships threading the archipelagoes,
My stars and stripes fluttering in the wind,
Commerce opening, the sleep of ages having done its work, races reborn, refresh'd,
Lives, works resumed—the object I know not—but the old, the Asiatic renew'd as it must be,
Commencing from this day surrounded by the world.

3

And you Libertad of the world!
You shall sit in the middle well-pois'd thousands and thousands of years,
As to-day from one side the nobles of Asia come to you,
As to-morrow from the other side the queen of England sends her eldest son to you.

The sign is reversing, the orb is enclosed,
The ring is circled, the journey is done,
The box-lid is but perceptibly open'd, nevertheless
the perfume pours copiously out of the whole
box.

Young Libertad! with the venerable Asia, the all-
mother,
Be considerate with her now and ever hot Libertad,
for you are all,
Bend your proud neck to the long-off mother now
sending messages over the archipelagoes to
you,
Bend your proud neck low for once, young Libertad.

Were the children straying westward so long? so
wide the tramping?
Were the precedent dim ages debouching westward
from Paradise so long?
Were the centuries steadily footing it that way, all
the while unknown, for you, for reasons?

They are justified, they are accomplish'd, they
shall now be turn'd the other way also, to
travel toward you thence,
They shall now also march obediently eastward for
your sake Libertad.

Walt Whitman

THE PRAIRIE STATES

A NEWER garden of creation, no primal solitude,
Dense, joyous, modern, populous millions, cities and farms,
With iron interlaced, composite, tied, many in one,
By all the world contributed—freedom's and law's and thrift's society,
The crown and teeming paradise, so far, of time's accumulations,
To justify the past.

IV

POEMS OF DEMOCRACY

TO FOREIGN LANDS

I HEARD that you ask'd for something to prove this
puzzle the New World,
And to define America, her athletic Democracy,
Therefore I send you my poems that you behold in
them what you wanted.

TO THEE OLD CAUSE

To THEE old cause!
Thou peerless, passionate, good cause,
Thou stern, remorseless, sweet idea,
Deathless throughout the ages, races, lands,
After a strange sad war, great war for thee
(I think all war through time was really fought, and
 ever will be really fought, for thee),
These chants for thee, the eternal march of thee.

(A war O soldiers not for itself alone,
Far, far more stood silently waiting behind, now to
 advance in this book.)

Thou orb of many orbs!
Thou seething principle! thou well-kept, latent
 germ! thou centre!
Around the idea of thee the war revolving,
With all its angry and vehement play of causes
(With vast results to come for thrice a thousand years),
These recitatives for thee,—my book and the war
 are one,
Merged in its spirit I and mine, as the contest
 hinged on thee,
As a wheel on its axis turns, this book unwitting to
 itself,
Around the idea of thee.

Walt Whitman

FOR YOU O DEMOCRACY

COME, I will make the continent indissoluble,
I will make the most splendid race the sun ever
    shone upon,
I will make divine magnetic lands,
  With the love of comrades,
    With the life-long love of comrades.

I will plant companionship thick as trees along all
  the rivers of America, and along the shores
  of the great lakes, and all over the prairies,
I will make inseparable cities with their arms about
    each other's necks,
  By the love of comrades,
    By the manly love of comrades.

For you these from me, O Democracy, to serve you
  ma femme!
For you, for you I am trilling these songs.

THOU MOTHER WITH THY EQUAL BROOD

1

THOU Mother with thy equal brood,
Thou varied chain of different States, yet one identity only,
A special song before I go I'd sing o'er all the rest,
For thee, the future.

I'd sow a seed for thee of endless Nationality,
I'd fashion thy ensemble including body and soul,
I'd show away ahead thy real Union, and how it may be accomplish'd.

The paths to the house I seek to make,
But leave to those to come the house itself.

Belief I sing, and preparation;
As Life and Nature are not great with reference to the present only,
But greater still from what is yet to come,
Out of that formula for thee I sing.

2

As a strong bird on pinions free,
Joyous, the amplest spaces heavenward cleaving,

Such be the thought I'd think of thee America,
Such be the recitative I'd bring for thee.

The conceits of the poets of other lands I'd bring thee not,
Nor the compliments that have served their turn so long,
Nor rhyme, nor the classics, nor perfume of foreign court or indoor library;
But an odour I'd bring as from forests of pine in Maine, or breath of an Illinois prairie,
With open airs of Virginia or Georgia or Tennessee, or from Texas uplands, or Florida's glades,
Or the Saguenay's black stream, or the wide blue spread of Huron,
With presentment of Yellowstone's scenes, or Yosemite,
And murmuring under, pervading all, I'd bring the rustling sea-sound,
That endlessly sounds from the two Great Seas of the world.

And for thy subtler sense subtler refrains dread Mother,
Preludes of intellect tallying these and thee, mind-formulas fitted for thee, real and sane and large as these and thee,
Thou! mounting higher, diving deeper than we knew, thou transcendental Union!

By thee fact to be justified, blended with thought,
Thought of man justified, blended with God,
Through thy idea, lo, the immortal reality!
Through thy reality, lo, the immortal idea!

3

Brain of the New World, what a task is thine,
To formulate the Modern—out of the peerless grandeur of the modern,
Out of thyself, comprising science, to recast poems, churches, art
(Recast, maybe discard them, end them—maybe their work is done, who knows?),
By vision, hand, conception, on the background of the mighty past, the dead,
To limn with absolute faith the mighty living present.

And yet thou living present brain, heir of the dead, the Old World brain,
Thou that lay folded like an unborn babe within its folds so long,
Thou carefully prepared by it so long—haply thou but unfoldest it, only maturest it,
It to eventuate in thee—the essence of the bygone time contain'd in thee,
Its poems, churches, arts, unwitting to themselves, destined with reference to thee;

Thou but the apples, long, long, long a-growing,
The fruit of all the Old ripening to-day in thee.

4

Sail, sail thy best, ship of Democracy,
Of value is thy freight, 'tis not the Present only,
The Past is also stored in thee,
Thou holdest not the venture of thyself alone, not
of the Western continent alone,
Earth's *résumé* entire floats on thy keel O ship,
is steadied by thy spars,
With thee Time voyages in trust, the antecedent
nations sink or swim with thee,
With all their ancient struggles, martyrs, heroes,
epics, wars, thou bear'st the other continents,
Theirs, theirs as much as thine, the destination-
port triumphant;
Steer then with good strong hand and wary eye O
helmsman, thou carriest great companions,
Venerable priestly Asia sails this day with thee,
And royal feudal Europe sails with thee.

5

Beautiful world of new superber birth that rises to
my eyes,
Like a limitless golden cloud filling the western sky,
Emblem of general maternity lifted above all,
Sacred shape of the bearer of daughters and sons,

Out of thy teeming womb thy giant babes in ceaseless procession issuing,
Acceding from such gestation, taking and giving continual strength and life,
World of the real—world of the twain in one,
World of the soul, born by the world of the real alone, led to identity, body, by it alone,
Yet in beginning only, incalculable masses of composite precious materials,
By history's cycles forwarded, by every nation, language, hither sent,
Ready, collected here, a freer, vast, electric world, to be constructed here
(The true New World, the world of orbic science, morals, literatures to come),
Thou wonder world yet undefined, unform'd, neither do I define thee,
How can I pierce the impenetrable blank of the future?
I feel thy ominous greatness evil as well as good,
I watch thee advancing, absorbing the present, transcending the past,
I see thy light lighting, and thy shadow shadowing, as if the entire globe,
But I do not undertake to define thee, hardly to comprehend thee,
I but thee name, thee prophesy, as now,
I merely thee ejaculate!

Thee in thy future,
Thee in thy only permanent life, career, thy own unloosen'd mind, thy soaring spirit,
Thee as another equally needed sun, radiant, ablaze, swift-moving, fructifying all,
Thee risen in potent cheerfulness and joy, in endless great hilarity,
Scattering for good the cloud that hung so long, that weigh'd so long upon the mind of man,
The doubt, suspicion, dread, of gradual, certain decadence of man;
Thee in thy larger, saner brood of female, male—thee in thy athletes, moral, spiritual, South, North, West, East,
(To thy immortal breasts, Mother of All, thy every daughter, son, endear'd alike, forever equal),
Thee in thy own musicians, singers, artists, unborn yet, but certain,
Thee in thy moral wealth and civilization (until which thy proudest material civilization must remain in vain),
Thee in thy all-supplying, all-enclosing worship—thee in no single bible, saviour, merely,
Thy saviours countless, latent within thyself, thy bibles incessant within thyself, equal to any, divine as any
(Thy soaring course thee formulating, not in thy two great wars, nor in thy century's visible growth,

But far more in these leaves and chants, thy chants,
great Mother!),
Thee in an education grown of thee, in teachers,
studies, students, born of thee,
Thee in thy democratic fêtes en-masse, thy high
original festivals, operas, lecturers, preachers,
Thee in thy ultimata (the preparations only now
completed, the edifice on sure foundations
tied),
Thee in thy pinnacles, intellect, thought, thy top-
most rational joys, thy love and godlike
aspiration,
In thy resplendent coming literati, thy full-lung'd
orators, thy sacerdotal bards, kosmic savans,
These! these in thee (certain to come), to-day I
prophesy.

6

Land tolerating all, accepting all, not for the good
alone, all good for thee,
Land in the realms of God to be a realm unto thyself,
Under the rule of God to be a rule unto thyself.

(Lo, where arise three peerless stars,
To be thy natal stars my country, Ensemble, Evo-
lution, Freedom,
Set in the sky of Law.)

Land of unprecedented faith, God's faith,

Thy soil, thy very subsoil, all upheav'd,
The general inner earth so long so sedulously draped
over, now hence for what it is boldly laid bare,
Open'd by thee to heaven's light for benefit or bale.

Not for success alone,
Not to fair-sail unintermitted always,
The storm shall dash thy face, the murk of war and
worse than war shall cover thee all over
(Wert capable of war, its tug and trials? be capable of peace, its trials,
For the tug and mortal strain of nations come at
last in prosperous peace, not war);
In many a smiling mask death shall approach beguiling thee, thou in disease shalt swelter,
The livid cancer spread its hideous claws, clinging
upon thy breasts, seeking to strike thee deep
within,
Consumption of the worst, moral consumption, shall
rouge thy face with hectic,
But thou shalt face thy fortunes, thy diseases, and
surmount them all,
Whatever they are to-day and whatever through
time they may be,
They each and all shall lift and pass away and
cease from thee,
While thou, Time's spirals rounding, out of thyself,
thyself still extricating, fusing,

Equable, natural, mystical Union thou (the mortal with immortal blent),
Shalt soar toward the fulfilment of the future, the spirit of the body and the mind,
The soul, its destinies.

The soul, its destinies, the real real
(Purport of all these apparitions of the real);
In thee America, the soul, its destinies,
Thou globe of globes! thou wonder nebulous!
By many a throe of heat and cold convuls'd (by these thyself solidifying),
Thou mental, moral orb—thou New, indeed new, Spiritual World!
The Present holds thee not—for such vast growth as thine,
For such unparallel'd flight as thine, such brood as thine,
The FUTURE only holds thee and can hold thee.

Walt Whitman

WHAT BEST I SEE IN THEE

To U. S. G. return'd from his World's Tour.

WHAT best I see in thee
Is not that where thou mov'st down history's great highways,
Ever undimm'd by time shoots warlike victory's dazzle,

Or that thou sat'st where Washington sat, ruling the land in peace,
Or thou the man whom feudal Europe fêted, venerable Asia swarm'd upon
Who walk'd with kings with even pace the round world's promenade;
But that in foreign lands, in all thy walks with kings,
Those prairie sovereigns of the West, Kansas, Missouri, Illinois,
Ohio's, Indiana's millions, comrades, farmers, soldiers, all to the front,
Invisibly with thee walking with kings with even pace the round world's promenade,
Were all so justified.

AS I WALK THESE BROAD MAJESTIC DAYS

As I walk these broad majestic days of peace
(For the war, the struggle of blood finish'd, wherein,
O terrific Ideal,
Against vast odds erewhile having gloriously won,
Now thou stridest on, yet perhaps in time toward
denser wars,
Perhaps to engage in time in still more dreadful
contests, dangers,
Longer campaigns and crises, labours beyond all
others),
Around me I hear that éclat of the world, politics,
produce,
The announcements of recognized things, science,
The approved growth of cities and the spread of
inventions.

I see the ships (they will last a few years),
The vast factories with their foremen and workmen,
And hear the indorsement of all, and do not object to
it.

But I too announce solid things,
Science, ships, politics, cities, factories, are not
nothing,

Like a grand procession to music of distant bugles
pouring, triumphantly moving, and grander
heaving in sight,
They stand for realities—all is as it should be.

Then my realities;
What else is so real as mine?
Libertad and the divine average, freedom to every
slave on the face of the earth,
The rapt promises and luminè of seers, the spiritual
world, these centuries-lasting songs,
And our visions, the visions of poets, the most solid
announcements of any.

THE UNITED STATES TO OLD WORLD CRITICS

HERE first the duties of to-day, the lessons of the
concrete,
Wealth, order, travel, shelter, products, plenty;
As of the building of some varied, vast, perpetual
edifice,
Whence to arise inevitable in time, the towering
roofs, the lamps,
The solid-planted spires tall shooting to the stars.

Walt Whitman

YEARS OF THE MODERN

YEARS of the modern! years of the unperform'd!
Your horizon rises, I see it parting away for more
 august dramas,
I see not America only, not only Liberty's nation
 but other nations preparing,
I see tremendous entrances and exits, new combi-
 nations, the solidarity of races,
The earth, restive, confronts a new era, perhaps a
 general divine war,
No one knows what will happen next, such portents
 fill the days and nights;
Years prophetical! the space ahead as I walk, as I
 vainly try to pierce it, is full of phantoms,
Unborn deeds, things soon to be, project their
 shapes around me,
This incredible rush and heat, this strange ecstatic
 fever of dreams O years!
Your dreams O years, how they penetrate through
 me! (I know not whether I sleep or wake.)
The perform'd America and Europe grow dim,
 retiring in shadow behind me,
The unperform'd, more gigantic than ever, advance,
 advance upon me.

O STAR OF FRANCE

1870-71

O STAR of France,
The brightness of thy hope and strength and fame,
Like some proud ship that led the fleet so long,
Beseems to-day a wreck driven by the gale, a mastless hulk,
And 'mid its teeming madden'd half-drown'd crowds,
Nor helm nor helmsman.

Dim smitten star,
Orb not of France alone, pale symbol of my soul its dearest hopes,
The struggle and the daring, rage divine for liberty,
Of aspirations toward the far ideal, enthusiast's dreams of brotherhood,
Of terror to the tyrant and the priest.

Star crucified—by traitors sold,
Star panting o'er a land of death, heroic land,
Strange, passionate, mocking, frivolous land.

Miserable! yet for thy errors, vanities, sins, I will not now rebuke thee,
Thy unexampled woes and pangs have quell'd them all,
And left thee sacred.

In that amid thy many faults thou ever aimedst highly,
In that thou wouldst not really sell thyself however great the price,
In that thou surely wakedst weeping from thy drugg'd sleep,
In that alone among thy sisters thou, giantess, didst rend the ones that shamed thee,
In that thou couldst not, wouldst not, wear the usual chains,
This cross, thy livid face, thy pierced hands and feet,
The spear thrust in thy side.

O star! O ship of France, beat back and baffled long!
Bear up O smitten orb! O ship continue on!

Sure as the ship of all, the Earth itself,
Product of deathly fire and turbulent chaos,
Forth from its spasms of fury and its poisons,
Issuing at last in perfect power and beauty,
Onward beneath the sun following its course,
So thee O ship of France

Finish'd the days, the clouds dispel'd,
The travail o'er, the long-sought extrication,

When lo! reborn, high o'er the European world,
(In gladness answering thence, as face afar to face,
 reflecting ours Columbia),
Again thy star O France, fair lustrous star,
In heavenly peace, clearer, more bright than ever,
Shall beam immortal.

Walt Whitman

THOUGHTS

I

Of these years I sing,
How they pass and have pass'd through convuls'd pains, as through parturitions,
How America illustrates birth, muscular youth, the promise, the sure fulfilment, the absolute success, despite of people—illustrates evil as well as good,
The vehement struggle so fierce for unity in one's-self;
How many hold despairingly yet to the models departed, caste, myths, obedience, compulsion, and to infidelity,
How few see the arrived models, the athletes, the Western States, or see freedom or spirituality, or hold any faith in results
(But I see the athletes, and I see the results of the war glorious and inevitable, and they again leading to other results).

How the great cities appear—how the Democratic masses, turbulent, wilful, as I love them,
How the whirl, the contest, the wrestle of evil with good, the sound and resounding, keep on and on,

How society waits unform'd, and is for a while between things ended and things begun,
How America is the continent of glories, and of the triumph of freedom and of the Democracies, and of the fruits of society, and of all that is begun,
And how the States are complete in themselves—and how all triumphs and glories are complete in themselves, to lead onward,
And how these of mine and of the States will in turn be convuls'd, and serve other parturitions and transitions,
And how all people, sights, combinations, the Democratic masses too, serve—and how every fact, and war itself, with all its horrors, serves,
And how now or at any time each serves the exquisite transition of death.

2

Of seeds dropping into the ground, of births,
Of the steady concentration of America, inland, upward, to impregnable and swarming places,
Of what Indiana, Kentucky, Arkansas, and the rest, are to be,
Of what a few years will show there in Nebraska, Colorado, Nevada, and the rest
(Or afar, mounting the Northern Pacific to Sitka or Aliaska),

Of what the feuillage of America is the preparation for—and of what all sights, North, South, East and West, are,
Of this Union welded in blood, of the solemn price paid, of the unnamed lost ever present in my mind;
Of the temporary use of materials for identity's sake,
Of the present, passing, departing—of the growth of completer men than any yet,
Of all sloping down there where the fresh free giver the mother, the Mississippi flows,
Of mighty inland cities yet unsurvey'd and unsuspected,
Of the new and good names, of the modern developments, of inalienable homesteads,
Of a free and original life there, of simple diet and clean and sweet blood,
Of litheness, majestic faces, clear eyes, and perfect physique there,
Of immense spiritual results future years far West, each side of the Anahuacs,
Of these songs, well understood there (being made for that area),
Of the native scorn of grossness and gain there
(O it lurks in me night and day—what is gain after all to savageness and freedom?).

BY BLUE ONTARIO'S SHORE

1

By blue Ontario's shore,
As I mused of these warlike days and of peace return'd, and the dead that return no more,
A Phantom gigantic superb, with stern visage accosted me,
Chant me the poem, it said, *that comes from the soul of America, chant me the carol of victory,*
And strike up the marches of Libertad, marches more powerful yet,
And sing me before you go the song of the throes of Democracy.

(Democracy, the destin'd conqueror, yet treacherous lip-smiles everywhere,
And death and infidelity at every step.)

2

A Nation announcing itself,
I myself make the only growth by which I can be appreciated,
I reject none, accept all, then reproduce all in my own forms.

A breed whose proof is in time and deeds,
What we are we are, nativity is answer enough to objections,

We wield ourselves as a weapon is wielded,
We are powerful and tremendous in ourselves,
We are executive in ourselves, we are sufficient in the variety of ourselves,
We are the most beautiful to ourselves and in ourselves,
We stand self-pois'd in the middle, branching thence over the world,
From Missouri, Nebraska, or Kansas, laughing attacks to scorn.

Nothing is sinful to us outside of ourselves,
Whatever appears, whatever does not appear, we are beautiful or sinful in ourselves only.

(O Mother—O Sisters dear!
If we are lost, no victor else has destroy'd us,
It is by ourselves we go down to eternal night.)

3

Have you thought there could be but a single supreme?
There can be any number of supremes—one does not countervail another any more than one eyesight countervails another, or one life countervails another.

All is eligible to all,
All is for individuals, all is for you,
No condition is prohibited, not God's or any.

All comes by the body, only health puts you rapport
with the universe.

Produce great Persons, the rest follows.

4

Piety and conformity to them that like,
Peace, obesity, allegiance, to them that like,
I am he who tauntingly compels men, women,
nations,
Crying, Leap from your seats and contend for your
lives!

I am he who walks the States with a barb'd tongue,
questioning every one I meet,
Who are you that wanted only to be told what you
knew before?
Who are you that wanted only a book to join you
in your nonsense?

(With pangs and cries as thine own O bearer of many
children,
These clamours wild to a race of pride I give.)

O lands, would you be freer than all that has ever
been before?
If you would be freer than all that has been before,
come listen to me.

Fear grace, elegance, civilization, delicatesse,
Fear the mellow sweet, the sucking of honey-juice,
Beware the advancing mortal ripening of Nature,
Beware what precedes the decay of the ruggedness of states and men.

5

Ages, precedents, have long been accumulating undirected materials,
America brings builders, and brings its own styles.

The immortal poets of Asia and Europe have done their work and pass'd to other spheres,
A work remains, the work of surpassing all they have done.

America, curious toward foreign characters, stands by its own at all hazards,
Stands removed, spacious, composite, sound, initiates the true use of precedents,
Does not repel them or the past or what they have produced under their forms,
Takes the lesson with calmness, perceives the corpse slowly borne from the house,
Perceives that it waits a little while in the door, that it was fittest for its days,
That its life has descended to the stalwart and well-shaped heir who approaches,
And that he shall be fittest for his days.

Any period one nation must lead,
One land must be the promise and reliance of the future.

These States are the amplest poem,
Here is not merely a nation but a teeming Nation of nations,
Here the doings of men correspond with the broadcast doings of the day and night,
Here is what moves in magnificent masses careless of particulars,
Here are the roughs, beards, friendliness, combativeness, the soul loves,
Here the flowing trains, here the crowds, equality, diversity, the soul loves.

6

Land of lands and bards to corroborate!
Of them standing among them, one lifts to the light a west-bred face,
To him the hereditary countenance bequeath'd both mother's and father's,
His first parts substances, earth, water, animals, trees,
Built of the common stock, having room for far and near,
Used to dispense with other lands, incarnating this land,

Attracting it body and soul to himself, hanging on
its neck with incomparable love,
Plunging his seminal muscle into its merits and
demerits,
Making its cities, beginnings, events, diversities,
wars, vocal in him,
Making its rivers, lakes, bays, embouchure in him,
Mississippi with yearly freshets and hanging chutes,
Columbia, Niagara, Hudson, spending themselves lovingly in him,
If the Atlantic coast stretch or the Pacific coast
stretch, he stretching with them North or
South,
Spanning between them East and West, and touching whatever is between them,
Growths growing from him to offset the growths of
pine, cedar, hemlock, live-oak, locust, chestnut, hickory, cottonwood, orange, magnolia,
Tangles as tangled in him as any canebrake or swamp,
He likening sides and peaks of mountains, forests
coated with northern transparent ice,
Off him pasturage sweet and natural as savanna,
upland, prairie,
Through him flights, whirls, screams, answering
those of the fish-hawk, mocking-bird, night-heron, and eagle,
His spirit surrounding his country's spirit, unclosed
to good and evil,

Surrounding the essences of real things, old times and present times,
Surrounding just found shores, islands, tribes of red aborigines,
Weather-beaten vessels, landings, settlements, embryo stature and muscle,
The haughty defiance of the Year One, war, peace, the formation of the Constitution,
The separate States, the simple elastic scheme, the immigrants,
The Union always swarming with blatherers and always sure and impregnable,
The unsurvey'd interior, log-houses, clearings, wild animals, hunters, trappers,
Surrounding the multiform agriculture, mines, temperature, the gestation of new States,
Congress convening every Twelfth-month, the members duly coming up from the uttermost parts,
Surrounding the noble character of mechanics and farmers, especially the young men,
Responding their manners, speech, dress, friendships, the gait they have of persons who never knew how it felt to stand in the presence of superiors,
The freshness and candor of their physiognomy, the copiousness and decision of their phrenology,
The picturesque looseness of their carriage, their fierceness when wrong'd,

The fluency of their speech, their delight in music, their curiosity, good temper and open-handdedness, the whole composite make,
The prevailing ardour and enterprise, the large amativeness,
The perfect equality of the female with the male, the fluid movement of the population,
The superior marine, free commerce, fisheries, whaling, gold-digging,
Wharf-hemm'd cities, railroad and steamboat lines intersecting all points,
Factories, mercantile life, labour-saving machinery, the Northeast, Northwest, Southwest,
Manhattan firemen, the Yankee swap, southern plantation life,
Slavery—the murderous, treacherous conspiracy to raise it upon the ruins of all the rest,
On and on to the grapple with it—Assassin! then your life or ours be the stake, and respite no more.

7

(Lo, high toward heaven, this day,
Libertad, from the conqueress' field return'd,
I mark the new aureola around your head,
No more of soft astral, but dazzling and fierce,
With war's flames and the lambent lightnings playing,

And your port immovable where you stand,
With still the inextinguishable glance and the clinch'd and lifted fist,
And your foot on the neck of the menacing one, the scorner utterly crush'd beneath you,
The menacing arrogant one that strode and advanced with his senseless scorn, bearing the murderous knife,
The wide-swelling one, the braggart that would yesterday do so much,
To-day a carrion dead and damn'd, the despised of all the earth,
An offal rank, to the dunghill maggots spurn'd.)

8

Others take finish, but the Republic is ever constructive and ever keeps vista,
Others adorn the past, but you O days of the present, I adorn you,
O days of the future I believe in you—I isolate myself for your sake,
O America because you build for mankind I build for you,
O well-beloved stone-cutters, I lead them who plan with decision and science,
Lead the present with friendly hand toward the future.

(Bravas to all impulses sending sane children to the next age!
But damn that which spends itself with no thought of the stain, pains, dismay, feebleness, it is bequeathing.)

9

I listened to the Phantom by Ontario's shore,
I heard the voice arising demanding bards,
By them all native and grand, by them alone can these States be fused into the compact organism of a nation.

To hold men together by paper and seal or by compulsion is no account,
That only holds men together which aggregates all in a living principle, as the hold of the limbs of the body or the fibres of plants.

Of all races and eras these States with veins full of poetical stuff most need poets, and are to have the greatest, and use them the greatest,
Their Presidents shall not be their common referee so much as their poets shall.

(Soul of love and tongue of fire:
Eye to pierce the deepest deeps and sweep the world!
Ah Mother, prolific and full in all besides, yet how long barren, barren?)

10

Of these States the poet is the equable man,
Not in him but off from him things are grotesque, eccentric, fail of their full returns,
Nothing out of its place is good, nothing in its place is bad,
He bestows on every object or quality its fit proportion, neither more nor less,
He is the arbiter of the diverse, he is the key,
He is the equalizer of his age and land,
He supplies what wants supplying, he checks what wants checking,
In peace out of him speaks the spirit of peace, large, rich, thrifty building populous towns, encouraging agriculture, arts, commerce, lighting the study of man, the soul, health, immortality, government,
In war he is the best backer of the war, he fetches artillery as good as the engineer's, he can make every word he speaks draw blood,
The years straying toward infidelity he withholds by his steady faith,
He is no arguer, he is judgment (Nature accepts him absolutely),
He judges not as the judges but as the sun falling round a helpless thing,
As he sees the farthest he has the most faith,
His thoughts are the hymns of the praise of things,

In the dispute on God and eternity he is silent,
He sees eternity less like a play with a prologue and dénouement,
He sees eternity in men and women, he does not see men and women as dreams or dots.

For the great Idea, the idea of perfect and free individuals,
For that, the bard walks in advance, leader of leaders,
The attitude of him cheers up slaves and horrifies foreign despots.

Without extinction is Liberty, without retrograde is Equality,
They live in the feelings of young men and the best women
(Not for nothing have the indomitable heads of the earth been always ready to fall for Liberty).

11

For the great Idea,
That, O my brethren, that is the mission of poets.

Songs of stern defiance ever ready,
Songs of the rapid arming and the march,
The flag of peace quick-folded, and instead the flag we know,
Warlike flag of the great Idea.

(Angry cloth I saw there leaping!
I stand again in leaden rain your flapping folds saluting,
I sing you over all, flying beckoning through the fight—O the hard-contested fight!
The cannons ope their rosy-flashing muzzles—the hurtled balls scream,
The battle-front forms amid the smoke—the volleys pour incessant from the line,
Hark, the ringing word *Charge!*—now the tussle and the furious maddening yells,
Now the corpses tumble curl'd upon the ground,
Cold, cold in death, for precious life of you,
Angry cloth I saw there leaping.)

12

Are you he who would assume a place to teach or be a poet here in the States?
The place is august, the terms obdurate.

Who would assume to teach here may well prepare himself body and mind,
He may well survey, ponder, arm, fortify, harden, make lithe himself,
He shall surely be question'd beforehand by me with many and stern questions.

Who are you indeed who would talk or sing to America?

Have you studied out the land, its idioms and men?
Have you learn'd the physiology, phrenology, politics, geography, pride, freedom, friendship of the land? its substratums and objects?
Have you consider'd the organic compact of the first day of the first year of Independence, sign'd by the Commissioners, ratified by the States, and read by Washington at the head of the army?
Have you possess'd yourself of the Federal Constitution?

Do you see who have left all feudal processes and poems behind them, and assumed the poems and processes of Democracy?
Are you faithful to things? do you teach what the land and sea, the bodies of men, womanhood, amativeness, heroic angers, teach?
Have you sped through fleeting customs, popularities?
Can you hold your hand against all seductions, follies, whirls, fierce contentions? are you very strong? are you really of the whole People?
Are you not of some coterie? some school or mere religion?
Are you done with reviews and criticisms of life? animating now to life itself?
Have you vivified yourself from the maternity of these States?

Have you too the old ever-fresh forbearance and impartiality?
Do you hold the like love for those hardening to maturity? for the last-born? little and big? and for the errant?

What is this you bring my America?
Is it uniform with my country?
Is it not something that has been better told or done before?
Have you not imported this or the spirit of it in some ship?
Is it not a mere tale? a rhyme? a prettiness?—is the good old cause in it?
Has it not dangled long at the heels of the poets, politicians, literats, of enemies' lands?
Does it not assume that what is notoriously gone is still here?
Does it answer universal needs? will it improve manners?
Does it sound with trumpet-voice the proud victory of the Union in that secession war?
Can your performance face the open fields and the seaside?
Will it absorb into me as I absorb food, air, to appear again in my strength, gait, face?
Have real employments contributed to it? original makers, not mere amanuenses?

Does it meet modern discoveries, calibres, facts, face
to face?

What does it mean to American persons, progresses,
cities? Chicago, Kanada, Arkansas?
Does it see behind the apparent custodians the real
custodians standing, menacing, silent, the mechanics, Manhattanese, Western men, Southerners, significant alike in their apathy, and
in the promptness of their love?
Does it see what finally befalls, and has always
finally befallen, each temporizer, patcher, outsider, partialist, alarmist, infidel, who has ever
ask'd any thing of America?
What mocking and scornful negligence?
The track strew'd with the dust of skeletons,
By the roadside others disdainfully toss'd.

13

Rhymes and rhymers pass away, poems distill'd from
poems pass away,
The swarms of reflectors and the polite pass, and
leave ashes,
Admirers, importers, obedient persons, make but the
soil of literature,
America justifies itself, give it time, no disguise can
deceive it or conceal from it, it is impassive
enough,

Only toward the likes of itself will it advance to meet them,
If its poets appear it will in due time advance to meet them, there is no fear of mistake
The proof of a poet shall be sternly deferr'd till his country absorbs him as affectionately as he has absorb'd it).

He masters whose spirit masters, he tastes sweetest who results sweetest in the long run,
The blood of the brawn beloved of time is unconstraint;
In the need of songs, philosophy, an appropriate native grand-opera, shipcraft, any craft,
He or she is greatest who contributes the greatest original practical example.

Already a nonchalant breed, silently emerging, appears on the streets,
People's lips salute only doers, lovers, satisfiers, positive knowers,
There will shortly be no more priests, I say their work is done,
Death is without emergencies here, but life is perpetual emergencies here,
Are your body, days, manners, superb? after death you shall be superb,

Justice, health, self-esteem, clear the way with irresistible power,
How dare you place any thing before a man?

14

Fall behind me States!
A man before all—myself, typical, before all.

Give me the pay I have served for,
Give to sing the songs of the great Idea, take all the rest,
I have loved the earth, sun, animals, I have despised riches,
I have given alms to every one that ask'd, stood up for the stupid and crazy, devoted my income and labour to others,
Hated tyrants, argued not concerning God, had patience and indulgence toward the people, taken off my hat to nothing known or unknown,
Gone freely with powerful uneducated persons and with the young, and with the mothers of families,
Read these leaves to myself in the open air, tried them by trees, stars, rivers,
Dismiss'd whatever insulted my own soul or defiled my body,

Claim'd nothing to myself which I have not carefully claim'd for others on the same terms,
Sped to the camps, and comrades found and accepted from every State
(Upon this breast has many a dying soldier lean'd to breathe his last,
This arm, this hand, this voice, have nourish'd, rais'd, restored,
To life recalling many a prostrate form);
I am willing to wait to be understood by the growth of the taste of myself,
Rejecting none, permitting all.

(Say O Mother, have I not to your thought been faithful?
Have I not through life kept you and yours before me?)

15

I swear I begin to see the meaning of these things,
It is not the earth, it is not America who is so great,
It is I who am great or to be great, it is You up there, or any one,
It is to walk rapidly through civilizations, governments, theories,
Through poems, pageants, shows, to form individuals.

Underneath all, undividuals,

I swear nothing is good to me now that ignores individuals,
The American compact is altogether with individuals,
The only government is that which makes minute of individuals,
The whole theory of the universe is directed unerringly to one single individual—namely to You.

(Mother! with subtle sense severe, with the naked sword in your hand,
I saw you at last refuse to treat but directly with individuals.)

16

Underneath all, Nativity,
I swear I will stand by my own nativity, pious or impious so be it;
I swear I am charm'd with nothing except nativity.
Men, women, cities, nations, are only beautiful from nativity.

Underneath all is the Expression of love for men and women
(I swear I have seen enough of mean and impotent modes of expressing love for men and women,
After this day I take my own modes of expressing love for men and women).

I swear I will have each quality of my race in myself
(Talk as you like, he only suits these States whose manners favour the audacity and sublime turbulence of the States).

Underneath the lessons of things, spirits, Nature, governments, ownerships, I swear I perceive other lessons,
Underneath all to me is myself, to you yourself (the same monotonous old song).

17

O I see flashing that this America is only you and me,
Its power, weapons, testimony, are you and me,
Its crimes, lies, thefts, defections, are you and me,
Its Congress is you and me, the officers, capitols, armies, ships, are you and me,
Its endless gestations of new States are you and me,
The war (that war so bloody and grim, the war I will henceforth forget) was you and me,
Natural and artificial are you and me,
Freedom, language, forms, employments, are you and me,
Past, present, future, are you and me.

I dare not shirk any part of myself,
Not any part of America good or bad,
Not to build for that which builds for mankind,

Not to balance ranks, complexions, creeds, and the
sexes,
Not to justify science nor the march of equality,
Nor to feed the arrogant blood of the brawn belov'd
of time.

I am for those that have never been master'd,
For men and women whose tempers have never been
master'd,
For those whom laws, theories, conventions, can
never master.

I am for those who walk abreast with the whole earth,
Who inaugurate one to inaugurate all.

I will not be outfaced by irrational things,
I will penetrate what it is in them that is sarcastic
upon me,
I will make cities and civilizations defer to me,
This is what I have learnt from America—it is the
amount, and it I teach again.

(Democracy, while weapons were everywhere aim'd
at your breast,
I saw you serenely give birth to immortal children,
saw in dreams you dilating form,
Saw you with spreading mantle covering the world.)

18

I will confront these shows of the day and night,
I will know if I am to be less than they,
I will see if I am not as majestic as they,
I will see if I am not as subtle and real as they,
I will see if I am to be less generous than they,
I will see if I have no meaning, while the houses and ships have meaning,
I will see if the fishes and birds are to be enough for themselves, and I am not to be enough for myself.

I match my spirit against yours you orbs, growths, mountains, brutes,
Copious as you are I absorb you all in myself, and become the master myself,
America isolated yet embodying all, what is it finally except myself?
These States, what are they except myself?

I know now why the earth is gross, tantalizing, wicked, it is for my sake,
I take you specially to be mine, you terrible, rude forms.

(Mother, bend down, bend close to me your face,
I know not what these plots and wars and deferments are for,

I know not fruition's success, but I know that
through war and crime your work goes on,
and must yet go on.)

19

Thus by blue Ontario's shore,
While the winds fann'd me and the waves came
trooping toward me,
I thrill'd with the power's pulsations, and the charm
of my theme was upon me,
Till the tissues that held me parted their ties upon
me.

And I saw the free souls of poets,
The loftiest bards of past ages strode before me,
Strange large men, long unwaked, undisclosed, were
disclosed to me.

20

O my rapt verse, my call, mock me not!
Not for the bards of the past, not to invoke them
have I launch'd you forth,
Not to call even those lofty bards here by Ontario's
shores,
Have I sung so capricious and loud my savage song.

Bards for my own land only I invoke
(For the war, the war is over, the field is clear'd),

Till they strike up marches henceforth triumphant
and onward,
To cheer O Mother your boundless expectant soul.

Bards of the great Idea! bards of the peaceful
inventions! (for the war, the war is over!)
Yet bards of latent armies, a million soldiers wait-
ing ever-ready,
Bards with songs as from burning coals or the
lightning's fork'd stripes!
Ample Ohio's, Kanada's bards—bards of Cali-
fornia! inland bards—bards of the war!
You by my charm I invoke.

EPILOGUE

RISE O DAYS FROM YOUR FATHOM-LESS DEEPS

RISE O DAYS FROM YOUR FATHOMLESS DEEPS

I

Rise O days from your fathomless deeps, till you loftier, fiercer sweep,
Long for my soul hungering gymnastic I devour'd what the earth gave me,
Long I roam'd the woods of the north, long I watch'd Niagara pouring,
I travel'd the prairies over and slept on their breast, I cross'd the Nevadas, I cross'd the plateaus,
I ascended the towering rocks along the Pacific, I sail'd out to sea,
I sail'd through the storm, I was refresh'd by the storm,
I watch'd with joy the threatening maws of the waves,
I mark'd the white combs where they career'd so high, curling over,
I heard the wind piping, I saw the black clouds,
Saw from below what arose and mounted (O superb! O wild as my heart, and powerful!),

Heard the continuous thunder as it bellow'd after
the lightning,
Noted the slender and jagged threads of lightning as
sudden and fast amid the din they chased
each other across the sky;
These, and such as these, I, elate, saw—saw with
wonder, yet pensive and masterful,
All the menacing might of the globe uprisen around
me,
Yet there with my soul I fed, I fed content, super-
cilious.

2

'Twas well, O soul—'twas a good preparation you
gave me,
Now we advance our latent and ampler hunger to fill,
Now we go forth to receive what the earth and the
sea never gave us,
Not through the mighty woods we go, but through
the mightier cities,
Something for us is pouring now more than Niagara
pouring,
Torrents of men (sources and rills of the North-
west are you indeed inexhaustible?),
What, to pavements and homesteads here, what
were those storms of the mountains and sea?
What, to passions I witness around me to-day? was
the sea risen?

Was the wind piping the pipe of death under the
black clouds?
Lo! from deeps more unfathomable, something more
deadly and savage,
Manhattan rising, advancing with menacing front—
Cincinnati, Chicago, unchain'd;
What was that swell I saw on the ocean? behold
what comes here,
How it climbs with daring feet and hands—how it
dashes!
How the true thunder bellows after the lightning—
how bright the flashes of lightning!
How Democracy with desperate vengeful port strides
on, shown through the dark by those flashes
of lightning!
(Yet a mournful wail and low sob I fancied I heard
through the dark,
In a lull of the deafening confusion.)

3

Thunder on! stride on, Democracy! strike with
vengeful stroke!
And do you rise higher than ever yet O days, O
cities!
Crash heavier, heavier yet O storms! you have done
me good,
My soul prepared in the mountains absorbs your
immortal strong nutriment,

Long had I walk'd my cities, my country roads
through farms, only half satisfied,
One doubt nauseous undulating like a snake,
crawl'd on the ground before me,
Continually preceding my steps, turning upon me
oft, ironically hissing low;
The cities I loved so well I abandon'd and left, I
sped to the certainties suitable to me,
Hungering, hungering, hungering, for primal ener-
gies and Nature's dauntlessness,
I refresh'd myself with it only, I could relish it
only,
I waited the bursting forth of the pent fire—on the
water and air I waited long;
But now I no longer wait, I am fully satisfied, I am
glutted,
I have witness'd the true lightning, I have witness'd
my cities electric,
I have lived to behold man burst forth and warlike
America rise,
Hence I will seek no more the food of the northern
solitary wilds,
No more the mountains roam or sail the stormy sea.

THE END